THE EASY LUNCH BOX

THE EASY
LUNCH BOX

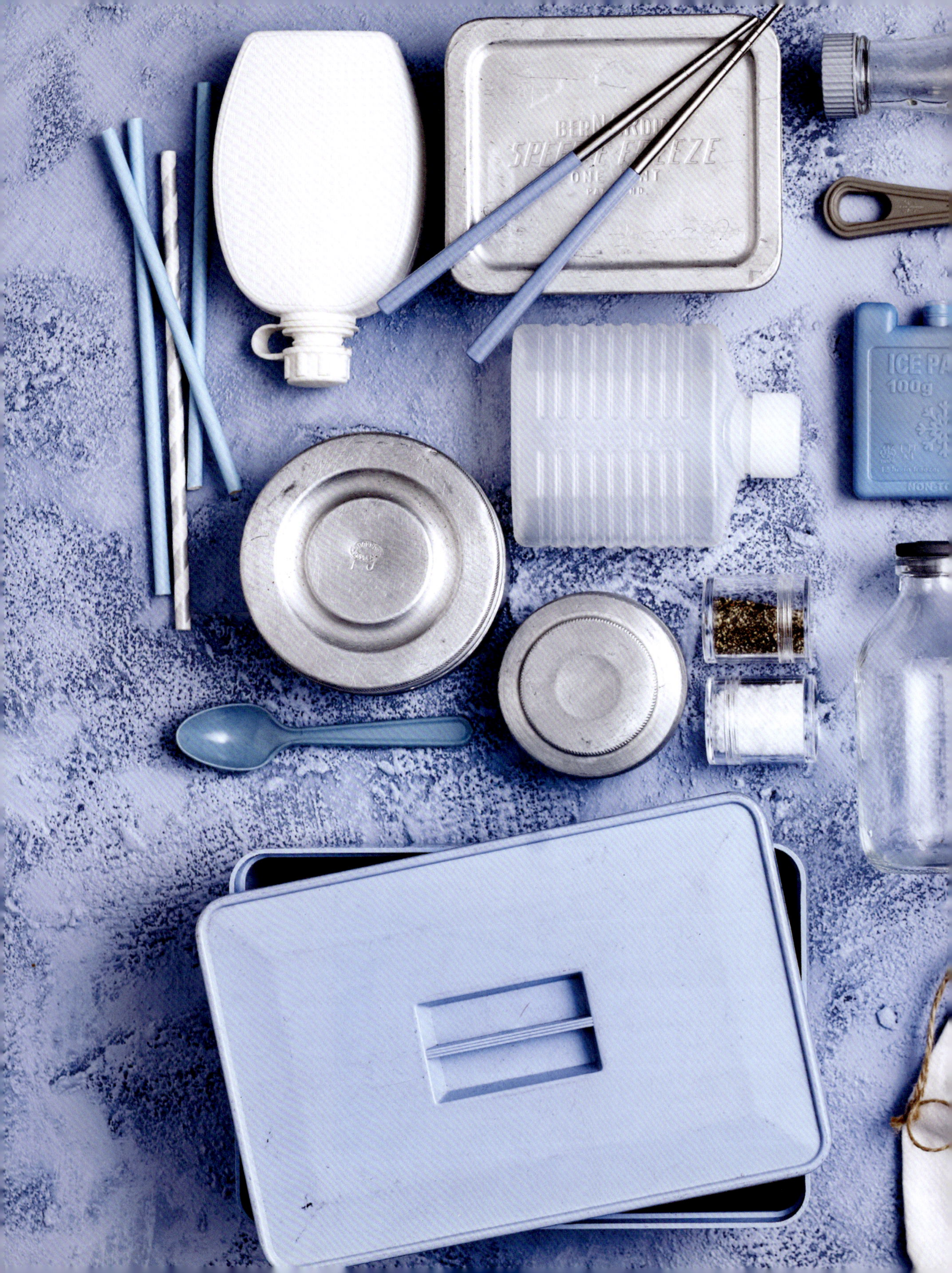
ICE PA
100g

CONTENTS

LET'S GET PACKING!

Home-made always beats store-bought, and with a little careful planning, you can pack a home-made lunch for work, uni or school every day. This saves you money, plus puts you in control of every ingredient and nutrient you eat.

No one likes, or deserves, a boring lunch. Whether you eat yours hunched over a work computer (tsk tsk), grab it between classes on campus, or you sit and eat it under a shady tree during lunch break, you need a meal full of nourishment and interest. The key is in thinking ahead – decide on next week's lunches over the weekend then shop for them all together, if that's practical.

DO-AHEAD HACKS

Consider other ways to reduce work by preparing ahead of time; here are just a few. Cut a week's worth of vegetable sticks (to eat with dips) on Sunday; they'll keep all week, portioned in containers. Bake double batches of muffins, cakes, scones, pastries etc. and freeze. Very finely slice root vegetables (beetroot, sweet potato and parsnips) and dry in the oven overnight at a low temperature for healthy crisps. Use your slow cooker or pressure cooker to make big batches of recipes you can use in lunches.

THE FREEZER IS YOUR FRIEND

It's a lifesaver to have lunches frozen, ready to go, and the extent of foods which can be frozen may surprise you. Many prepared sandwiches will freeze, including those filled with grated cheese, peanut butter, ham, salami and roast meats. Mustards, pickles, mayo and chutneys will freeze well too. Pies, quiches, pizza, cakes and sweet slices can be pre-portioned and frozen, and muffins and scones freeze brilliantly too. Have plenty of different types of breads, wraps and rolls on hand in the freezer to make your sandwiches.

USE LEFTOVERS

Utilise leftovers (when there are any) from dinner the night before; roast chicken and other meats make excellent sandwich fillings and leftover roast or grilled vegetables can form the basis of a delicious salad, for example. Cook extra food for dinner so you have excess for lunches – use extra meats and vegetables for sandwich fillings or extra pasta, rice or other grains for a salad. Get creative; leftover bolognese sauce, curry, home-made baked beans or a meat-based casserole can be baked in puff pastry to make easy hand pies for lunch. Leftover breakfast can also be repurposed for the lunch box; combine cooled, excess porridge with yoghurt, honey and chopped fruits for a nutritious treat. Or roll leftover pancakes around a lightly sweetened ricotta and strawberry filling. The possibilities are endless, with a little creative thinking.

SAFETY & TRANSPORT

Lunch boxes come in many different styles and sizes, and in a range of materials, from plastic and nylon to stainless steel. It's important to have the right kind of box to protect your food and keep it safely at the right temperature.

Food safety is the biggest concern with a packed lunch. If it's not stored properly for the few hours before you eat it, bacteria can grow. Meat and dairy products are particularly prone. Other high risk foods include fish, poultry, eggs and anything packaged in a jar or can, which can become high risk once opened. This is especially the case concerning children as they can be more susceptible to food poisoning. Keeping foods cool is the key to food safety. If you don't have a lunch box that can be chilled, throw a frozen ice-pack in with your packed box to keep food as cool as possible.

Freezing a plastic bottle of water or juice will perform the same function and makes for a refreshingly chilled drink by the time lunchtime comes around too. Even using frozen bread slices to make sandwiches, and packing baked goods straight from the freezer, will keep things chilled for just that extra bit longer. The lowest risk foods for spoilage include uncooked fruits and vegetables, dried foods (crackers, biscuits and other baked goods) and pre-packaged foods such as cereal bars, dried fruits and popcorn.

TYPES OF LUNCH BOXES

CLASSIC BOXES

Boxes run the gamut of simple, economical supermarket buys to smart canvas bag-like boxes with multiple compartments. One size doesn't fit all. What works in summer may not work in winter; for example, boxes with a little ventilation are important for warmer ambient temperatures as food more readily overheats and sweats when tightly enclosed.

BENTO BOXES

Boxes with different compartments are excellent when you need to separate your salad from your dips and your cheese from your chocolate cake. With this type of box there is no need to wrap foods, meaning less plastic. Stainless steel is a great material as it is sturdy and washes well, without retaining food odours and taints, as plastic can.

THERMOS FLASK

Invest in a thermos flask to hold food at the right temperature for hours. It will keep soups, pasta, baked beans etc. hot, and yoghurt, chilled soups and desserts safely cold for up to 6 hours. There are also freezable poly-canvas lunch bags with water-resistant lining, which you freeze overnight. These keep foods fresh for hours, without having to add a separate ice-pack.

SNACKS

AIR FRYER BREAKFAST COOKIES

PREP + COOK TIME 50 minutes

MAKES 26

STORE IT Breakfast cookies will keep in an airtight container for up to 2 weeks, or freeze them for up to 2 months.

2 cups (180g) rolled oats
½ cup (75g) sunflower seeds
½ cup (40g) flaked almonds
½ cup (50g) pepitas
1¼ cups (175g) dried pitted dates, chopped finely
2 tbsp extra virgin olive oil
1¼ cups (350g) dark roast crunchy peanut butter
1 tsp ground cinnamon
2 egg whites
olive oil cooking spray
⅓ cup (115g) golden syrup, warmed

1 Line a 7-litre air fryer basket with baking paper. Place oats, sunflower seeds, almonds and pepitas in the basket (there is no need to preheat the air fryer); at 160°C, cook for 12 minutes, stirring halfway through, or until golden.

2 Meanwhile, place dates in a large heatproof bowl and cover with ½ cup (125ml) boiling water; stand for 5 minutes. Whisk in oil, peanut butter, cinnamon and egg whites while still warm.

3 Tip the hot oat mixture over the peanut butter mixture; immediately stir vigorously to combine well.

4 Preheat the air fryer to 150°C for 5 minutes.

5 Roll 2 tbsp of mixture into 26 balls using oiled hands; place 5cm apart on a tray lined with baking paper. Flatten balls into 6cm rounds with the palm of your hand. Spray the air fryer basket with cooking spray.

6 Taking care, place 9 cookie rounds in the basket, slightly apart (cookies will not spread); at 150°C, cook for 10 minutes or until dark golden and cooked through. Carefully transfer cookies to a wire rack and brush immediately with warm golden syrup. Repeat cooking two more times with remaining cookie rounds and golden syrup. Cool.

AIR
FRYER

AIR
FRYER

AIR FRYER YAKI ONIGIRI (GRILLED RICE BALLS)

PREP + COOK TIME 50 minutes (+ cooling)

MAKES 10

TIP Shichimi togarashi is a spicy Japanese condiment made with dried chilli, sesame seeds, nori flakes and several other spices. You'll find it in the Asian section of supermarkets or at Asian grocers.

PREP IT Onigiri can be made 1 day ahead. Store in an airtight container in the fridge.

2 cups (360g) sushi rice, rinsed until water runs clear
190g canned tuna in springwater, drained
⅓ cup (100g) kewpie (Japanese) mayonnaise
¼ cup (50g) frozen corn kernels, thawed
1 green onion, sliced thinly
olive oil cooking spray
¼ cup (60ml) teriyaki sauce
2 nori sheets
extra kewpie (Japanese) mayonnaise sprinkled with shichimi togarashi (see tip), to serve

1 Place rice and 3 cups (750ml) water in a medium saucepan; bring to a simmer. Cover with lid; cook on low heat for 20 minutes. Remove from heat and set aside, covered, for 20 minutes. Remove lid and cool to room temperature.

2 Meanwhile, combine tuna, mayonnaise, corn and green onion in a medium bowl; season to taste.

3 Preheat a 7-litre air fryer to 180°C for 3 minutes.

4 Using damp hands, place ⅓ cup (80g) cooked rice in the palm of one hand and make an indent in the centre; place 1 heaped tsp of filling in the hollow and enclose to form a ball. Shape the ball into a triangle. Repeat with remaining rice and filling to make 10 onigiri in total. Spray onigiri on both sides with cooking spray.

5 Taking care, place onigiri in the air fryer basket; at 180°C, cook for 12 minutes, turning halfway through cooking, or until just crisp. Brush lightly with teriyaki sauce; cook for a further 2 minutes. Turn onigiri over and brush with a little more teriyaki sauce; cook for another 2 minutes or until crisp and golden.

6 Slice nori into ten 3cm x 10cm strips. Brush with a little water, then fold around the base of each onigiri.

7 Serve onigiri with extra kewpie mayonnaise sprinkled with shichimi togarashi.

AIR FRYER CRISPY BBQ CHICKPEAS

PREP + COOK TIME 25 minutes

MAKES 2 cups

STORE IT Crispy chickpeas can be stored in an airtight container for up to 1 week. To refresh, place in the air fryer basket and spray with olive oil cooking spray. Cook in a preheated air fryer at 180°C for 4 minutes.

2 x 400g cans chickpeas drained, rinsed
2 tbsp extra virgin olive oil
2 tbsp barbecue seasoning powder
2 tbsp sunflower seeds
2 tbsp pepitas

1 Preheat a 7-litre air fryer to 180°C for 3 minutes.

2 Place chickpeas on a tray lined with paper towel; pat with more paper towel until well dried.

3 Combine oil and barbecue seasoning in a large bowl; add chickpeas and toss to coat.

4 Taking care, place chickpeas in the air fryer basket; at 180°C, cook for 12 minutes, tossing halfway through cooking. Add the seeds; cook for a further 6 minutes or until chickpeas are crisp and golden.

5 Serve immediately or cool completely, then store.

MAKE
AHEAD
AIR
FRYER

FREEZER
FRIENDLY
AIR
FRYER

AIR FRYER CHEESY PESTO SCROLLS

PREP + COOK TIME 50 minutes (+ freezing)

MAKES 12

SWAP IT Homemade pesto can be replaced with ¼ cup (65g) bottled basil or sun-dried tomato pesto.

FREEZE IT Cheesy pesto scrolls can be frozen, individually wrapped in plastic, for up to 1 month. Pack them in your lunch container frozen; they'll be defrosted by lunch time. Otherwise, thaw in fridge before reheating.

1 cup firmly packed basil leaves
1 clove garlic, chopped
2 tbsp pine nuts, toasted
2 tbsp finely grated parmesan
¼ cup (60ml) extra virgin olive oil
1 tbsp lemon juice
2 cups (300g) self-raising flour
1 tsp fine salt
1 tbsp caster sugar
50g cold butter, chopped coarsely
¾ cup (180ml) milk, approximately
1 cup (120g) grated pizza cheese

1 Process basil, garlic, pine nuts and parmesan in a food processor until chopped finely. With motor operating, gradually add combined oil and lemon juice until pesto is almost smooth; season to taste.

2 Sift flour and salt into a medium bowl; stir in sugar. Using your fingers, rub in butter. Add enough milk to form a soft, sticky dough. Turn dough out onto a lightly floured sheet of baking paper; knead lightly until smooth. Sprinkle paper with more flour, if necessary. Roll dough out to a 30cm x 40cm rectangle.

3 Spread dough evenly with the pesto; scatter over pizza cheese. Roll dough up tightly from the long side to form a log; place log in the freezer for 10 minutes to firm slightly.

4 Preheat a 7-litre air fryer to 160°C for 5 minutes.

5 Using a serrated knife, trim ends off the log; cut log into 12 slices.

6 Taking care, line the air fryer basket with baking paper. Place scrolls, cut-side up, in the basket, then cover basket tightly with foil; at 160°C, cook for 10 minutes.

7 Remove foil; cook for a further 10 minutes until scrolls are golden and cooked through.

8 Serve scrolls warm or cold.

AIR FRYER HEALTHIER TORTILLA CHIPS WITH GUACAMOLE

PREP + COOK TIME 30 minutes

SERVES 4

PREP IT Guacamole can be made a day ahead; cover directly with plastic wrap to prevent browning and refrigerate. Tortilla chips can be made 2 days ahead and stored in an airtight container.

312g packet white corn tortillas (gluten free)
1 tsp ground cumin
1 tsp smoked paprika
1 tsp salt flakes
olive oil cooking spray

SPECIAL GUACAMOLE
2 medium avocados (500g)
1 small red chilli, chopped finely (optional)
¼ tsp ground cumin
1 small clove garlic, crushed
2 tbsp lime juice
½ cup finely chopped coriander (cilantro) to serve
Tabasco chipotle sauce, coriander sprigs and lime wedges, to serve

1 Preheat a 5.3-litre air fryer to 200°C for 3 minutes.

2 Stack three tortillas on top of each other, then cut the stack into six wedges. Repeat with remaining tortillas.

3 Combine cumin, paprika and salt flakes in a small bowl.

4 Taking care, place a third of the tortilla wedges in the air fryer basket; at 200°C, cook for 7 minutes, turning halfway through cooking time, until crisp. Transfer to a platter; spray with oil and sprinkle with a third of the spice mix. Repeat with remaining tortilla wedges, oil spray and spice mix.

5 Meanwhile, make special guacamole: Using a spoon, scoop the flesh from avocados into a bowl. Add half the chilli, and remaining ingredients; mash together using a potato masher or fork to form a chunky texture. Season to taste.

6 Top guacamole with remaining chilli, chipotle sauce and coriander sprigs. Serve with tortilla chips and lime wedges.

GLUTEN FREE
AIR FRYER

MAKE
AHEAD

SWEET POTATO DIP

PREP + COOK TIME 25 minutes

MAKES 3½ cups

PREP IT Dip can be made up to 3 days ahead; store in an airtight container in the fridge.

PACK IT Spoon dip into a small airtight container. Pack with your choice of dippers in a cooler bag to keep cool.

1 tbsp extra virgin olive oil
5 green onions, chopped
1 clove garlic, crushed
1 tbsp finely chopped coriander stems
1 tsp ground cumin
1 tsp ground coriander
1 tsp harissa paste
4 medium carrots (500g), grated coarsely
1 small orange sweet potato (250g), grated coarsely
½ cup (125ml) vegetable or chicken stock
400g can cannellini beans, drained, rinsed
crisp pitta chips, snow peas, sugar snap peas, baby cucumbers, celery sticks and sliced capsicum, to serve

1 Heat oil in a large heavy-based saucepan over medium-high heat; cook green onion, garlic, coriander stems and ground spices for 1 minute. Add harissa, carrot and sweet potato; cook, stirring, for 2 minutes. Add stock; bring to the boil. Reduce heat to low; cook, covered, for 5 minutes or until vegetables soften.

2 Transfer vegetable mixture to a food processor with beans; process until smooth. Season to taste. Cool.

3 Serve dip with crisp pitta chips, snow peas, sugar snap peas, baby cucumbers, celery sticks and sliced capsicum.

HAM & CORN CUPS

PREP + COOK TIME 40 minutes (+ cooling)

MAKES 12

PREP IT Cups can be made up to 2 days ahead; store in an airtight container in the fridge.

FREEZE IT Individual cups can be frozen, wrapped in plastic wrap, for up to 1 month. Pack in your lunch container frozen; it will be defrosted by lunch time. Otherwise, thaw in the fridge before reheating.

12 slices gluten-free white bread
4 eggs
¼ cup (60ml) milk
200g sliced gluten-free leg ham, chopped
125g can corn kernels, drained
⅓ cup (40g) grated tasty cheese
2 tbsp finely chopped chives

1 Preheat oven to 180°C/160°C fan-forced. Grease a 12-hole (⅓-cup/80ml) muffin pan.

2 Trim crusts from bread slices. Roll bread with a rolling pin to flatten. Using a 9cm round cutter, cut a round from each slice of bread; press rounds into pan holes. Bake for 4 minutes or until bread is dry. (Bread should not be brown at this stage.) Cool in pan.

3 Meanwhile, whisk eggs and milk in a jug; season.

4 Combine ham, corn, cheese and half the chives in a medium bowl.

5 Divide ham mixture evenly among bread cups in pan holes; pour over egg mixture. Bake for 25 minutes or until egg is just set and bread is browned lightly. Leave in pan for 5 minutes to cool slightly.

6 Sprinkle cups with remaining chives to serve.

GLUTEN FREE
FREEZER FRIENDLY

PASTRY TWISTS

CHEESIE TWIGGY TWISTS

PREP + COOK TIME 12 minutes **MAKES** 8

Preheat a 5.3-litre air fryer to 200°C for 3 minutes. Cut 1 sheet partially thawed butter puff pastry into eight 1.5cm x 20cm strips. Squeeze a thin line of American mustard along the middle of each strip. Using four 40g packets mild salami and tasty cheese Stix, cut each piece of cheese and salami in half lengthways. Stack a cheese half on top of a salami half, then wrap each stack with a strip of pastry, mustard-side down, to form a spiral. Brush pastry with egg wash; sprinkle with a pinch of dried oregano and chilli flakes. Taking care, line the air fryer basket with baking paper and place twists in the basket; cook for 6 minutes or until puffed and golden. Stand for 5 minutes, then serve with spicy tomato relish.

CHERRY PINWHEELS

PREP + COOK TIME 30 minutes (+ standing & freezing) **MAKES** 9

Combine ⅓ cup (40g) ground almonds, 1½ tbsp sugar and 2 tbsp melted butter in a small bowl; stand for 10 minutes. Cut 1 sheet partially thawed butter puff pastry into nine squares. Make a 3cm cut from the corner of each square towards the centre; place 2 tsp of almond mixture in centre of each pastry. Fold every second point into the middle to form a pinwheel. Place pastries in the freezer for 30 minutes to firm. Preheat a 5.3-litre air fryer to 200°C for 3 minutes. Brush pastries with egg wash. Spoon ½ tsp cherry jam in the centre of each pastry; top with a thawed frozen or a canned cherry. Spray the air fryer basket with cooking oil spray. Taking care, place half the pastries in the basket; cook for 10 minutes or until puffed and golden. Repeat cooking remaining pastries, spraying the basket with more cooking oil spray. Transfer to a wire rack to cool.

CARAMEL NUT SPIRALS

PREP + COOK TIME 20 minutes (+ freezing) **MAKES** 10

Spread 1 sheet partially thawed butter puff pastry with 2½ tbsp caramel spread, leaving a 3mm border. Scatter with 2 tbsp ground hazelnuts and a large pinch of ground allspice. Place another pastry sheet on top, pressing together gently. Place pastry in the freezer for 30 minutes to firm, then cut into 10 even strips. Pinch one end of a strip and twist from that end to the other end five times. Holding one end of the strip flat on a work surface, wrap strip around to form a twisted spiral. Brush pastry with egg wash. Repeat with remaining pastry strips. Preheat a 5.3-litre air fryer to 180°C for 3 minutes. Taking care, line the air fryer basket with baking paper and place pastries in the basket; cook for 12 minutes or until puffed and golden. Transfer to a wire rack to cool. Drizzle with extra caramel spread.

RED PESTO SCROLLS

PREP + COOK TIME 30 minutes (+ freezing) **MAKES** 12

Combine ½ cup (120g) spreadable cream cheese, 2 tbsp each red pesto and grated parmesan and 1 tbsp chopped flat-leaf parsley. Spread mixture over 1 sheet partially thawed butter puff pastry, spreading right to the edges. Roll one edge into the middle of the sheet and stop, then repeat with the opposite side to meet in the middle. Place pastry in the freezer for 30 minutes to firm. Preheat a 5.3-litre air fryer to 180°C for 3 minutes. Cut rolled pastry into 2cm thick strips. Brush a cut side of each pastry with egg wash and sprinkle with a little extra grated parmesan. Taking care, line the air fryer basket with baking paper and place pastries, cheese-side up, in the basket; cook for 10 minutes or until puffed and golden. Transfer to a wire rack to cool.

AIR
FRYER

FREEZER
FRIENDLY

CHEAT'S CHEESY RICE BALLS

PREP + COOK TIME 50 minutes

MAKES 24

PREP IT Rice balls can be made up to 3 days ahead; store in an airtight container in the fridge.

FREEZE IT Rice balls can be frozen in an airtight container for up to 2 months; thaw in the fridge before reheating.

2 cups (500ml) vegetable stock
450g packet microwave long grain rice
1 cup (100g) pizza cheese
½ cup (40g) finely grated parmesan
3 eggs
2 tbsp flat-leaf parsley leaves, chopped finely
1½ cups (115g) panko breadcrumbs
vegetable oil, for deep-frying

1 Place stock and rice in a medium saucepan; bring to the boil over high heat. Reduce heat to medium; cook, covered, stirring occasionally to separate rice grains, for 5 minutes or until rice is soft. Remove from heat. Stand for 5 minutes; drain. Cool slightly. Transfer to a heatproof bowl.

2 Add cheeses, 1 egg and the parsley to rice; mix well to combine. Season to taste. Roll 1½-tbsp portions of rice mixture into balls to make 24 in total.

3 Place remaining eggs and the breadcrumbs in separate shallow bowls. Lightly beat eggs. Coat rice balls in egg then in breadcrumbs.

4 Heat oil in a deep medium-sized heavy-based saucepan until 180°C (or until the base of a wooden spoon bubbles when placed in the oil). Cook rice balls, in batches, for 4 minutes or until crisp and golden. Drain on paper towel.

HALOUMI, RISONI & ZUCCHINI SLICE

PREP + COOK TIME
1 hour 10 minutes (+ cooling)

MAKES 16

PREP IT Slice can be made up to 2 days ahead; wrap individual pieces in baking paper then plastic wrap and store in an airtight container in the fridge.

FREEZE IT Individual pieces can be frozen, between sheets of baking paper, in an airtight container for up to 2 months.

1 cup (220g) risoni
4 medium zucchini (500g), grated coarsely
½ tsp finely grated lemon rind
250g haloumi, grated coarsely
4 green onions, chopped finely
1 clove garlic, crushed
⅓ cup (25g) finely grated parmesan
2 tbsp finely chopped flat-leaf parsley
4 eggs, beaten lightly
½ cup (75g) self-raising flour

1 Cook risoni in a saucepan of boiling salted water for 8 minutes or until just tender; drain. Cool.

2 Preheat oven to 180°C/160°C fan-forced. Grease a 20cm x 30cm slice pan; line base and sides with baking paper, extending paper 5cm over long sides.

3 Squeeze as much liquid from zucchini as possible; transfer to a large bowl. Add risoni, lemon rind, half the haloumi, the green onion, garlic, parmesan, parsley and egg; stir to combine. Add flour; stir well to combine. Season.

4 Pour mixture into prepared pan, smoothing the surface; scatter with remaining haloumi. Bake for 45 minutes or until firm, golden and cooked through. Leave in pan for 15 minutes before cutting into 16 pieces.

made
WITH LOVE
FREEZER
FRIENDLY

FAST
FREEZER FRIENDLY

PROTEIN BALLS

PREP TIME 15 minutes (+ refrigeration)

MAKES 24

STORE IT Protein balls can be stored in an airtight container in the fridge for up to 1 week or freezer for up to 2 months; thaw in the fridge.

2 cups (180g) traditional rolled oats
1 cup (75g) shredded coconut
1 cup (280g) peanut butter
1 cup finely chopped pitted fresh medjool dates
½ cup (100g) pepitas, chopped coarsely
½ cup (60g) coarsely chopped pecans
¼ cup (40g) chia seeds
¼ cup (60g) coconut oil
1 tbsp cacao powder
1 tsp vanilla extract
½ tsp ground cinnamon
⅓ cup (40g) sesame seeds or ½ cup (25g) cacao powder

1 Combine all ingredients, except sesame seeds, in a large bowl; mix well with your hands.

2 Using damp hands, roll 1-tbsp portions of mixture into balls, pressing firmly together, to make 24 in total.

3 Roll in sesame seeds or cacao powder to coat. Place balls on a baking-paper-lined tray. Cover tray with plastic wrap. Refrigerate until ready to eat.

SESAME SEED SNAPS

PREP + COOK TIME 20 minutes (+ standing)

MAKES 16

STORE IT Sesame seed snaps can be stored in an airtight container for up to 2 weeks.

2⅓ cups (300g) sesame seeds
½ cup (100g) pepitas
⅓ cup (65g) dried sweetened cranberries
1 cup (360g) honey

1 Grease a 23cm x 33cm slice pan; line base and sides with baking paper, extending paper 2cm over long sides.

2 Combine sesame seeds and pepitas in a large frying pan over low heat; cook, stirring continuously, for 5 minutes or until sesame seeds are light brown. Stir in cranberries. Remove pan from heat.

3 Heat honey in a medium saucepan over medium heat until just starting to boil; add sesame seed mixture and cook, stirring, for 5 minutes until golden brown.

4 Carefully pour seed mixture into prepared pan; smooth the top using the back of a large spoon. Place a sheet of baking paper over the top, then a baking tray large enough to fit inside the slice pan; gently press to flatten and compress (this will ensure a smooth and even slice). Stand at room temperature for 30 minutes or until firm.

5 Transfer slice to a chopping board and cut into 16 even-sized pieces.

GLUTEN
FREE

MAKE
AHEAD

MUFFINS

MEXICAN

PREP + COOK TIME 40 minutes **MAKES** 10

Make Basic Muffin (see recipe, below), adding 2 tsp taco spice mix, ½ small coarsely chopped red capsicum, ⅓ cup drained canned corn kernels and 2 tbsp coarsely chopped coriander leaves to muffin mixture; season. Spoon mixture into pan holes. Continue with recipe. Serve muffins topped with 1 small diced avocado.

BASIC MUFFIN

PREP + COOK TIME 35 minutes **MAKES** 10

Preheat oven to 200°C/180°C fan-forced. Grease 10 holes of a 12-hole (⅓-cup/80ml) muffin pan. Sift 2 cups self-raising flour into a bowl. Whisk 80g melted butter, 1 cup (250ml) buttermilk and 1 lightly beaten egg in a jug; season. Stir wet ingredients into flour until just combined (do not overmix; the mixture should be lumpy). Spoon muffin mixture into pan holes. Bake for 25 minutes or until a skewer inserted into the centre of one comes out clean. Leave in pan for 5 minutes; transfer to a wire rack to cool.

AMERICAN

PREP + COOK TIME 40 minutes **MAKES** 10

Make Basic Muffin (see recipe, below left), adding 2 tbsp mild american mustard to wet ingredients. Spoon mixture into pan holes. Cut 3 burger cheese slices into quarters; slice 5 cocktail frankfurts into 4 pieces each. Top each muffin with a piece of cheese and 2 frankfurt slices, pressing in slightly. Continue with recipe. Serve topped with ⅓ cup drained bread & butter pickles, american mustard and tomato sauce.

MEDITERRANEAN

PREP + COOK TIME 40 minutes **MAKES** 10

Make Basic Muffin (see recipe, left), adding ¼ cup thinly sliced semi-sundried tomatoes, ¼ cup chopped green olives, ¼ cup chopped drained roasted capsicum, 1 tbsp finely chopped basil and ⅔ cup finely grated parmesan to muffin mixture; season. Spoon mixture into pan holes. Top with an extra ¼ cup thinly sliced semi-sundried tomatoes and 2 tbsp chopped green olives. Continue with recipe.

FRUIT SALAD RICE PAPER ROLLS

PREP TIME 30 MINUTES

SERVES 6 (MAKES 12 ROLLS)

TIPS We used 15cm diameter rice paper rounds here. They are available from major supermarkets and Asian food stores. Be sure to use ripe fruit for this recipe, as they give the best flavour.

12 small rice paper rounds (60g) (see tips)
½ small red papaya (200g), sliced thinly
2 medium kiwifruit (170g), sliced thinly
125g small strawberries, halved
125g raspberries, halved
½ cup mint leaves

HONEY LIME DIPPING SAUCE
2 limes (130g)
2 tbsp honey

1 Make honey lime dipping sauce: Finely grate rind from the limes. Juice limes; you will need ⅓ cup. Place lime rind, juice and honey in a small bowl; whisk to combine.

2 Cover a chopping board with a damp clean tea towel. Place one rice paper round at a time in a bowl of warm water until softened. Place on tea towel; top rice paper with one-twelfth of the sliced papaya, kiwifruit, strawberry, raspberry and mint leaves in a line along the centre of the sheet. Fold bottom half of the rice paper over to enclose fruit, then fold in both sides; roll over to enclose the filling completely.

3 Repeat with remaining rice paper rounds, fruit and mint to make a total of 12 rolls. Place rolls on a plastic-wrap-lined tray; cover with damp paper towel. Refrigerate until ready to serve.

4 Serve rice paper rolls with dipping sauce, sprinkled with extra mint leaves, if you like.

FREEZER FRIENDLY
AIR FRYER

AIR FRYER CHEWY APRICOT SEED BARS

PREP + COOK TIME 35 minutes

MAKES 18

STORE IT Bars can be stored in an airtight container for up to 1 week, or freeze them for up to 2 months.

⅓ cup (50g) plain flour
½ tsp mixed spice
3 cups (270g) quick cook rolled oats
⅔ cup (50g) desiccated coconut
150g natural seed mix
125g dried apricots, chopped finely
200g unsalted butter, chopped
½ cup (175g) golden syrup
¾ cup (165g) firmly packed brown sugar
⅓ cup (95g) crunchy peanut butter
1 tsp vanilla extract

1 Preheat a 7-litre air fryer to 160°C for 5 minutes. Grease a deep 20cm square cake pan; line base and sides with two layers of baking paper.

2 Sift flour and mixed spice into a large bowl. Add oats, coconut, seed mix and apricots; stir to combine.

3 Place butter and golden syrup in a small saucepan; stir over low heat until melted. Add sugar, peanut butter and vanilla, stirring until combined. Stir butter mixture into flour mixture until well combined. Press mixture evenly into cake pan.

4 Taking care, place cake pan in the air fryer basket; at 160°C, cook for 25 minutes or until golden brown and firm. Cool in pan before cutting into 18 bars.

FAST

LOADED HUMMUS

POMEGRANATE & PINE NUT

PREP TIME 10 minutes **SERVES** 4

Stir 1 tsp ground cumin into a 200g tub of hummus until combined. Spoon hummus into 4 sealable containers. Scatter pomegranate seeds, toasted pine nuts and thinly sliced red onion over hummus; season to taste. Drizzle with extra virgin olive oil.

HARISSA & CHICKPEA

PREP + COOK TIME 25 minutes **SERVES** 4

Spoon a 200g tub of hummus into 4 sealable containers. Preheat oven to 200°C/180°C fan-forced. Pat a drained and rinsed 400g can chickpeas dry with paper towel, then place in a bowl. Add 1 tbsp each harissa and olive oil; stir to combine. Spread chickpea mixture, in a single layer, on a baking-paper-lined oven tray. Bake in oven, stirring three times during cooking, for 20 minutes or until well browned and slightly crunchy. Scatter chickpea mixture and small mint leaves evenly over hummus in containers; season to taste. Drizzle with extra virgin olive oil.

SPICED CRUNCH

PREP + COOK TIME 5 minutes **SERVES** 4

Spoon a 200g tub of hummus into 4 sealable containers. Heat 2 tbsp olive oil in a small frying pan over medium heat; cook 2 tbsp pepitas and 1 tsp each cumin seeds, sesame seeds and crushed coriander seeds, stirring, until toasted. Scatter seed mixture and thin strips of lemon rind evenly over hummus in containers. Drizzle each with extra virgin olive oil.

GREEK SALAD

PREP TIME 10 minutes **SERVES** 4

Spoon a 200g tub of hummus into 4 sealable containers. Combine 1 tbsp each of finely diced cucumber, ripe tomato, red onion, crumbled fetta and chopped pitted kalamata olives. Scatter evenly over hummus in containers; sprinkle with dried Greek-style oregano and season to taste. Drizzle with extra virgin olive oil.

COLD STUFF

TUNA NICOISE WRAPS

PREP + COOK TIME 20 minutes (+ cooling)

MAKES 2

PREP IT Cook eggs the day before; store in an airtight container in the fridge. Assemble wraps in the morning or the day before; refrigerate in an airtight lunch container. Keep chilled until ready to eat.

2 eggs
50g green beans, trimmed
2 gluten-free wraps
6 baby gem lettuce leaves, trimmed
2 x 125g cans tuna slices in springwater, drained
8 cherry tomatoes, quartered
¼ cup (40g) pitted kalamata olives, halved
⅓ cup (80ml) store-bought yoghurt fetta dill dressing (optional)

1 Place eggs in a small saucepan; cover with cold water. Bring to the boil over high heat; boil for 6 minutes. Drain; cool. Peel eggs and cut into quarters.

2 Boil, steam or microwave beans until just tender; drain. Rinse under cold water; drain. Cut in half lengthways.

3 Place wraps on a chopping board. Divide lettuce leaves, tuna, tomatoes, beans, olives and egg between wraps; drizzle with dressing and season. Wrap up tightly to enclose filling.

GLUTEN
FREE

FAST

CHEESE & SALAMI LUNCH ROLLS

PREP + COOK TIME 20 minutes

MAKES 4

TIP Chargrilled mixed peppers are available from major supermarkets, use roasted or char-grilled red capsicum instead, if preferred.

PREP IT Make lunch rolls the day before; store in an airtight container in the fridge until ready to pack into a lunch container.

280g jar mixed chargrilled peppers (see tip)
4 sourdough rolls
200g spreadable cream cheese
50g shaved mild salami
4 slices Swiss cheese, cut into quarters
2 large tomatoes, sliced thinly
40g baby rocket leaves

1 Drain peppers and pat dry with paper towel. Using a serrated knife, cut the top off from each roll, approximately 2cm from top; reserve roll tops. Gently remove the inside bread from each roll, leaving approximately a 1cm border all the way around.

2 Spread cream cheese over the inside base and top of each roll. Layer inside the rolls with half the salami, cheese, peppers, tomato and rocket. Repeat layering one more time with remaining ingredients, finishing with the rocket.

3 Top each roll with the reserved roll tops; press down gently. Cut rolls in half. Serve straight away or refrigerate until required.

EGG NORI ROLLS

PREP + COOK TIME 20 minutes

SERVES 4

PREP IT Cook omelettes the day before; store, covered, in the fridge. Cut cucumber and carrot the day before, store in an airtight container in the fridge.

PACK IT Assemble nori rolls in the morning; refrigerate in an airtight lunch container. Pack pickled ginger and soy sauce in a separate small airtight container. Keep chilled until ready to eat.

8 eggs
1 lebanese cucumber
1 medium carrot
1 medium avocado
4 rye mountain bread wraps
⅓ cup (100g) kewpie (Japanese) mayonnaise
4 sheets toasted seaweed (nori)
pickled ginger and soy sauce, to serve (optional)

1 Whisk eggs and ⅓ cup (80ml) water in a large jug until well combined.

2 Heat a lightly oiled 26cm non-stick frying pan over medium heat. Pour a quarter of the egg mixture into pan; cook, tilting pan, until omelette is just set. Remove from pan. Repeat with remaining egg mixture to make four omelettes in total. Cool.

3 Meanwhile, cut cucumber in quarters lengthways; remove seeds, then cut into thin strips. Trim carrot; cut into thin batons. Cut avocado into thin slices lengthways.

4 Place wraps on a chopping board; spread evenly with mayonnaise, then top with a nori sheet and an omelette, trimming omelette where necessary so it's the same size as the wrap. Place cucumber, carrot and avocado along the long edge of each wrap; roll up firmly to enclose filling, then trim ends. Cut each roll crossways into four pieces. Serve rolls with pickled ginger and soy sauce.

FAST

CLUB SANDWICHES

PREP + COOK TIME 30 minutes

SERVES 2

PREP IT Make chicken mixture the day before; store, covered, in the fridge.

PACK IT Assemble sandwiches in the morning; store in an airtight container in the fridge. Keep chilled until ready to eat.

500g chicken tenderloins
1 tbsp olive oil
3 rindless bacon rashers
¼ cup (75g) whole-egg mayonnaise
½ stalk celery, sliced thinly
4 slices wholemeal bread
2 slices white bread
1 baby cos lettuce, leaves separated
1 large tomato, sliced thinly

1 Place chicken on a chopping board; using a rolling pin, flatten slightly so they're all the same thickness (this will allow the chicken to cook evenly).

2 Heat half the oil in a medium non-stick frying pan over medium-high heat. Cook the bacon for 3 minutes or until crisp; drain on paper towel. Cut each rasher in half.

3 Heat remaining oil in the same pan over medium heat; cook chicken for 3 minutes each side or until cooked through. When cool enough to handle, chop coarsely.

4 Combine chicken, mayonnaise and celery in a bowl.

5 Toast bread slices until lightly browned.

6 Spread chicken mixture on 2 slices of wholemeal toast; top with white toast, then top white toast with lettuce, bacon, tomato and remaining wholemeal toast. Cut each sandwich in half.

CHICKPEA WRAPS

PREP + COOK TIME 40 minutes

MAKES 4

SWAP IT Use store-bought pumpkin hummus or your favourite hummus instead of making your own.

PREP IT Make pumpkin hummus the day before; store in an airtight container in the fridge. (Pumpkin hummus will keep in the fridge for up to 1 week.) Assemble wraps in the morning or the day before; store in an airtight container in the fridge. Keep chilled until ready to eat.

4 wholegrain wraps
1 baby cos lettuce, leaves separated
1 stalk celery, sliced
1 small red capsicum, sliced thinly
1 lebanese cucumber, sliced into ribbons
125g can corn kernels, drained
200g store-bought lightly salted crispy chickpeas

PUMPKIN HUMMUS
400g butternut pumpkin, cut into 2cm pieces
2 cloves garlic, unpeeled
½ cup (125ml) extra virgin olive oil
400g can chickpeas, drained, rinsed
2 tbsp tahini paste
2 tbsp lemon juice
1 tsp sea salt flakes

1 To make pumpkin hummus: Preheat oven to 200°C/180°C fan-forced. Place pumpkin and garlic on an oven tray; drizzle with 2 tbsps of the oil and stir to combine. Bake for 20 minutes or until tender. Cool slightly; reserve pan juices. Squeeze garlic from skins; discard skins. Blend or process pumpkin, garlic and reserved pan juices with remaining ingredients and 2 tbsp water until smooth.

2 Place wraps on a chopping board; spread evenly with hummus. Divide lettuce leaves, celery, capsicum, cucumber, corn and chickpeas among wraps. Fold in sides and wrap up tightly to enclose filling.

FAST

SMOKED TURKEY & BRIE SANDWICHES

PREP TIME 10 minutes

MAKES 2

SWAP IT Use Dijonnaise instead of combining the mayonnaise and Dijon mustard yourself.

PREP IT Make sandwiches in the morning or the night before. Store in an airtight lunch container in the fridge. Keep chilled until ready to eat.

4 slices light rye bread
1 tbsp cranberry sauce
50g brie, sliced thinly
1 cup (50g) baby spinach leaves
1 large vine-ripened tomato, sliced thinly
80g smoked turkey slices
1½ tbsp whole-egg mayonnaise
1 tsp Dijon mustard

1 Lay bread slices on a chopping board. Divide cranberry sauce, brie, spinach, tomato and turkey between two of the bread slices. Season to taste.

2 Combine mayonnaise and Dijon mustard in a small bowl.

3 Spread remaining bread slices with the Dijon mayonnaise and place on top of filling; cut sandwiches in half.

JAPANESE-STYLE TUNA SALAD

PREP TIME 20 minutes

SERVES 4

SWAP IT Use 2 x 250g packets microwave brown rice & quinoa instead of brown rice and 2 x 125g cans salmon slices in springwater instead of tuna.

PREP IT Prepare rice to the end of step 2 the day before; store in an airtight container in the fridge.

PACK IT In the morning, continue from step 3: Pack rice and tuna mixture, sprinkled with sesame seeds, in an airtight container, and remaining dressing and the mayonnaise in separate airtight containers. Keep chilled until ready to eat.

450g packet microwave brown rice
⅔ cup (160ml) store-bought Japanese sesame & soy dressing
2 x 125g cans tuna slices in springwater, drained
1 lebanese cucumber, sliced
1 small avocado, quartered
1 large carrot, julienned
100g snow peas, trimmed, sliced thinly
⅓ cup (90g) drained pickled ginger
⅓ cup (100g) kewpie (Japanese) mayonnaise
1 tbsp white sesame seeds

1 Heat rice following packet instructions.

2 Add half the dressing to warm rice; stir to combine. Cool.

3 Top rice with tuna, cucumber, avocado, carrot, snow peas and pickled ginger.

4 Just before serving, drizzle with remaining dressing, top with mayonnaise and sprinkle with sesame seeds.

CHICKEN MEATBALL & CRISPY NOODLE SALAD

PREP + COOK TIME 35 minutes

SERVES 4

PREP IT Make meatballs the day before. Make crispy noodle salad, without dressing, the day before. Store meatballs and noodle salad in separate airtight containers in the fridge.

PACK IT In the morning, assemble salad in an airtight lunch container; pack dressing in a separate airtight container. Keep chilled until ready to eat.

500g chicken mince
⅔ cup (50g) fresh breadcrumbs
1 egg
1 small onion, grated coarsely
¼ cup finely chopped flat-leaf parsley leaves, plus extra to serve
2 tbsp olive oil
200g snow peas, trimmed
2 cups finely shredded wombok
300g can corn kernels, drained
1 large red capsicum, chopped
100g packet fried noodles
½ cup (125ml) store-bought oriental salad dressing

1 Place chicken, breadcrumbs, egg, onion and parsley in a medium bowl; season. Mix well to combine. Roll level tbsps of mixture into 24 balls.

2 Heat oil in a large frying pan over medium heat; cook meatballs, in batches, turning, for 8 minutes or until browned and cooked through.

3 Meanwhile, place snow peas in a heatproof bowl, pour boiling water over and stand for 2 minute; drain. Refesh in iced water. Slice thinly.

4 Arrange wombok in a large bowl; top with corn, snow peas, capsicum and meatballs. Scatter over fried noodles and extra parsley. Drizzle over dressing.

ROAST VEG & QUINOA SALAD

PREP + COOK TIME 40 minutes

SERVES 4

SWAP IT Use sweet potato instead of pumpkin, couscous instead of quinoa and baby kale leaves instead of rocket.

PREP IT Make salad, without adding the rocket and dressing, the day before; store salad in an airtight container in the fridge. Refrigerate dressing in its jar.

PACK IT In the morning, toss rocket through salad and pack dressing in a separate airtight container. Keep chilled until ready to eat

500g butternut pumpkin, cut into 3cm pieces
1 medium red capsicum, sliced thinly
2 small zucchini, chopped
1 bunch mixed baby carrots, trimmed, peeled
1 small red onion, cut into thin wedges
2 tbsp olive oil
¼ cup Moroccan seasoning
1 cup (200g) white quinoa, rinsed
60g baby rocket leaves
200g fetta, crumbled

LEMON DRESSING
¼ cup (60ml) olive oil
2 tbsp lemon juice

1 Preheat oven to 200°C/180°C fan-forced. Line a large oven tray with baking paper.

2 Place pumpkin, capsicum, zucchini, carrots and onion on tray; drizzle with oil. Sprinkle with seasoning and toss to combine; season. Roast for 25 minutes or until vegetables are tender and browned.

3 Meanwhile, place quinoa and 1½ cups (375ml) water in a medium saucepan over high heat; bring to the boil. Reduce heat to low; cook, covered, for 8 minutes or until most of the liquid absorbs. Stand, covered, for 10 minutes. Drain.

4 Make lemon dressing: Place ingredients in a screw-top jar; season to taste. Shake well.

5 Place quinoa, roasted vegetables, rocket and dressing in a large bowl; toss to combine. Top with fetta; season to taste.

TWISTED TUNA ROLLS

TUNA & AVOCADO CAESAR ROLL

PREP TIME 10 minutes **MAKES** 1

Mix a drained 125g can tuna in oil with 1 tbsp caesar dressing and 1 tsp finely grated parmesan. Butter a bread roll. Top base with baby cos leaves, then tuna mixture, sliced avocado and sliced ripe tomato. Season to taste; serve. Add crisp prosciutto, if you like.

TUNA & ROASTED CAPSICUM SUB

PREP TIME 10 minutes **MAKES** 1

Mix a drained 125g can tuna in oil with 1 tbsp aïoli, 2 tsp finely chopped basil and 2 tsp chopped toasted pine nuts or sunflower seeds (or 2 tsp pesto instead of the basil and pine nuts). Butter a split long crusty bread roll. Fill roll with trimmed rocket leaves and tuna mixture; top with drained marinated capsicum strips. Season to taste.

TUNA 'SUSHI' SUB

PREP TIME 10 minutes **MAKES** 1

Mix a drained 125g can tuna in oil with 1 tbsp Japanese mayonnaise and sriracha chilli sauce to taste. Butter a split long crusty bread roll. Fill roll with Lebanese cucumber ribbons, tuna mixture and thinly sliced radish. Season to taste.

MEXICAN TUNA SALAD ROLL

PREP TIME 10 minutes **MAKES** 1

Mix a drained 125g can tuna in oil with 1 tbsp whole-egg mayonnaise, a little finely chopped red onion, finely chopped coriander, 1 tbsp drained canned corn and chipotle Tabasco sauce to taste. Butter a ciabatta bread roll. Top base with watercress, then tuna mixture and coriander leaves. Season to taste.

FAST
YUM

TWISTED PASTA SALAD

PREP + COOK TIME 20 minutes

SERVES 4

SWAP IT Use your favourite pasta type or rice instead of fusilli.

PREP IT Make pasta salad to the end of step 2 the day before; store in an airtight container. Make dressing the day before; store in its jar in the fridge.

PACK IT In the morning, combine salad and dressing; portion into an airtight lunch container. Keep chilled until ready to eat.

375g fusilli pasta
1 medium green capsicum, chopped
½ cup (60g) sliced kalamata olives, drained
110g baby bocconcini, torn
150g cabanossi, sliced
250g cherry tomatoes, quartered

DIJON DRESSING
¼ cup (60ml) extra virgin olive oil
2 tbsp lemon juice
2 tsp Dijon mustard

1 Cook pasta in a medium saucepan of salted boiling water following packet instructions until just tender; drain. Cool.

2 Place cooled pasta in a large bowl with capsicum, olives, bocconcini, cabanossi and tomatoes; toss to combine.

3 Make Dijon dressing: Place ingredients in a screw-top jar; season to taste. Shake well.

4 Add dressing to pasta salad, toss well. Season to taste.

LAMB KOFTA SALAD

PREP + COOK TIME 30 minutes (+ refrigeration)

SERVES 4 (MAKES 8 KOFTAS)

PREP IT Make koftas to the end of step 2 the day before; store in an airtight container in the fridge. Make dressing the day before; refrigerate in its jar.

PACK IT In the morning, assemble koftas and salad mixture in an airtight lunch container. Pack the dip and tortilla strips in separate airtight containers. Keep chilled until ready to eat.

½ cup mint leaves
500g lamb mince
1 tbsp ground cumin
1 tbsp ground sumac
2 cloves garlic, crushed
1 tbsp olive oil
80g mixed salad leaves
1 Lebanese cucumber, diced
250g cherry tomatoes, quartered
½ small red onion, sliced thinly
200g fetta, crumbled
200g tub store-bought tzatziki dip
tortilla strips, to serve

LEMON DRESSING
¼ cup (60ml) olive oil
2 tbsp lemon juice

1 Finely chop 1 tbsp of the mint leaves; reserve remaining leaves. Combine lamb, cumin, sumac, garlic and chopped mint in a medium bowl; season. Using your hands, combine mixture well. Divide mixture into eight portions; shape each portion into a sausage shape. Cover; refrigerate for 1 hour.

2 Heat oil in a large non-stick frying pan over medium-high heat. Cook koftas, turning, for 6 minutes or until browned all over and cooked through.

3 Make lemon dressing; Place ingredients in a screw-top jar; season to taste. Shake well.

4 Combine salad leaves, cucumber, tomatoes, onion, fetta and remaining mint leaves in a large bowl; drizzle over dressing.

5 Serve koftas with salad, tzatziki and tortilla strips.

FAST

VEGIE POKE BOWL

PREP + COOK TIME 20 minutes

SERVES 4

SWAP IT Use noodles instead of brown rice.

PREP IT Prepare the recipe to the end of step 3 the day before; store salad ingredients, rice mixture and omelette ribbons in separate airtight containers in the fridge.

PACK IT In the morning, assemble rice mixture, salad ingredients, omelette ribbons, nori sprinkles and extra sesame seeds; portion into an airtight lunch container. Pack remaining dressing in a separate airtight container. Keep chilled until ready to eat.

2 x 250g packets microwave brown rice
½ cup (125ml) store-bought Japanese sesame soy dressing
4 eggs
¼ cup (60ml) milk
1 tbsp sesame seeds, toasted, plus extra to serve
1 cup (80g) shredded wombok
1 cup (80g) shredded red cabbage
200g frozen shelled edamame
1 telegraph cucumber, sliced
8 radishes, trimmed, halved
8 baby carrots, trimmed, halved lengthways
nori sprinkles, to serve (optional)

1 Heat rice following packet instructions; transfer to a large bowl. Add half the dressing to warm rice; stir to combine. Cool.

2 Whisk eggs, milk and sesame seeds in a large jug until well combined.

3 Heat a lightly oiled wok or medium non-stick frying pan over high heat. Pour half the egg mixture into wok; cook, tilting wok, to form a 20cm round. Cook for 1 minute or until just set; transfer to a plate. Repeat with remaining egg mixture to make two omelettes. Cool slightly. Roll each omelette into a log, then thinly slice into ribbons.

4 Serve rice mixture with wombok, cabbage, edamame, cucumber, radishes and carrots; drizzle with remaining dressing. Top with egg ribbons and sprinkle with nori and extra sesame seeds.

SALMON, BARLEY & TAHINI GREENS SALAD

PREP + COOK TIME 35 minutes

SERVES 2

PREP IT Prepare the salad to the end of step 4 the night before; store salad and dressing in separate airtight containers in the fridge.

PACK IT Portion salad into an airtight lunch container. Pack dressing in a separate airtight container. Keep chilled until ready to eat.

¾ cup (150g) pearl barley, rinsed
1 cup (250ml) vegetable stock
200g green beans, trimmed, halved
100g sugar snap peas
1 bunch cavolo nero, stalks removed, chopped coarsely
300g hot-smoked salmon, torn into pieces
2 tbsp white sesame seeds, toasted

TAHINI DRESSING
2 tbsp extra virgin olive oil
1 tbsp tahini
½ tsp finely grated lime rind
1½ tbsp lime juice
2 tsp honey
1 tsp Dijon mustard
1 tsp boiling water

1 Place barley, stock and ½ cup (125ml) water in a large heavy-based saucepan with a tight-fitting lid. Bring to the boil over high heat; reduce heat to low. Cook, covered, for 25 minutes or until barley is just tender.

2 Meanwhile, make tahini dressing; Place ingredients in a jug or bowl; whisk until smooth, thick and emulsified. Add more boiling water, if necessary, to achieve the desired consistency. Season to taste. (Makes ½ cup.)

3 Return heat to high; season barley well with salt and add vegetables. Cook, covered, for 3 minutes or until beans and sugar snap peas are just cooked through and cavolo nero wilts. Drain.

4 Combine the barley mixture and salmon pieces; scatter with sesame seeds.

5 Just before serving, spoon dressing over salad.

GINGER BEEF & QUINOA SALAD

PREP + COOK TIME 35 minutes

SERVES 2

PREP IT Prepare recipe to the end of step 5 the day before. Store beef mixture and quinoa salad mixture in separate airtight containers in the fridge. Refrigerate dressing in its jar.

PACK IT In the morning, combine quinoa salad mixture and beef mixture; portion into an airtight lunch container. Pack dressing in a separate container. Keep refrigerated until ready to eat.

½ cup (100g) tri-coloured quinoa, rinsed well
2 tsp fish sauce
2cm piece fresh ginger, grated finely
1 small clove garlic, crushed
¼ tsp freshly ground black pepper
200g beef fillet steak
100g sugar snap peas, trimmed, halved lengthways
1 baby gem lettuce, quartered
½ butter lettuce, leaves separated
1 trimmed celery stalk, sliced thinly on the diagonal
2 green onions, sliced thinly lengthways
1 fresh long red chilli, sliced thinly (optional)
lime wedges, to serve

LIME & GINGER DRESSING
2 tbsp lime juice
2 tbsp extra virgin olive oil
2cm piece fresh ginger, grated finely
1 fresh long red chilli, seeded, chopped finely (optional)

1 Place quinoa and 1 cup (250ml) water in a medium saucepan over high heat; bring to the boil. Reduce heat to low; cook, covered, for 12 minutes or until most of the liquid is absorbed. Stand, covered, for 10 minutes. Fluff with a fork.

2 Meanwhile, place fish sauce, ginger, garlic and pepper in a small bowl; stir to combine. Coat beef with ginger mixture. Cook beef in an oiled heavy-based frying pan over high heat, turning, for 4 minutes for medium or until cooked to your liking. Transfer to a plate; cover loosely with foil and stand for 5 minutes. Slice thinly.

3 Meanwhile, boil, steam or microwave sugar snap peas until just tender; drain. Cool slightly.

4 Place quinoa, lettuce leaves, celery and cooled peas in a large bowl; toss to combine.

5 Make lime and ginger dressing: Place ingredients in a screw-top jar; season to taste. Shake well.

6 Add dressing to salad and toss to combine; top with beef. Scatter with green onion and chilli; serve with lime wedges.

TUNA & TOMATO SALAD

PREP + COOK TIME 20 minutes

SERVES 2

PREP IT Prepare the recipe to the end of step 2 the night before. Store eggs in the fridge. Refrigerate dressing, covered.

PACK IT Place salad ingredients and quartered eggs into airtight lunch containers. Pack tuna can. Pack the dressing in a separate airtight container or a jar. Keep refrigerated until ready to eat.

2 eggs
2 tbsp extra virgin olive oil
½ tsp finely grated lemon rind
1½ tbsp lemon juice
1 tsp wholegrain mustard
½ tsp caster sugar
2 tsp finely chopped chives
4 cocktail truss tomatoes, sliced
120g yellow grape tomatoes, halved
4 baby cucumbers (qukes), halved lengthways, sliced thickly
2 x 125g cans tuna slices in oil, drained

1 Place eggs in a saucepan of cold water; bring to a simmer. Cook for 5 minutes for soft-boiled, 7 minutes for medium-boiled or 9 minutes for hard-boiled. Cool immediately under cold water. Refrigerate until required.

2 For the dressing, whisk oil, rind, lemon juice, mustard, sugar and half the chives in a small bowl or screw-top jar. Season to taste.

3 Combine tomato, cucumber and remaining chives; divide between two lunch containers. Peel and quarter eggs; add to salads.

4 Before serving, add tuna slices to salad and drizzle with dressing. Season to taste.

FAST

FAST

CRUNCHY CHICKEN & EGG SALAD

PREP + COOK TIME 25 minutes

SERVES 2

PREP IT Prepare the recipe to the end of step 3 the night before. Store salad in an airtight container in the fridge.

PACK IT Pack salad, dressing and bread in separate airtight containers. Keep refrigerated until ready to eat.

2 tbsp extra virgin olive oil
1 chicken breast fillet, halved horizontally
2 eggs
100g mixed salad leaves
2 roma tomatoes, chopped
2 slices wholegrain sourdough bread
⅓ cup (100g) caesar dressing

1 Heat oil in a large non-stick frying pan over medium heat. Cook chicken for 4 minutes on each side or until golden and cooked through. Cover loosely with foil; cool. Slice chicken.

2 Meanwhile, place eggs in a saucepan of cold water; bring to a simmer. Cook for 5 minutes for soft-boiled or until cooked to your liking. Cool; peel and quarter.

3 Combine leaves, tomatoes, egg and chicken in a bowl.

4 To make the croutons, toast sourdough in a toaster until crisp and golden. Tear into bite-sized pieces.

5 Before serving, scatter croutons over salad; spoon over dressing. Season to taste.

FARRO, TOMATO & AVOCADO SALAD JARS

PREP + COOK TIME 40 minutes

SERVES 4

PREP IT Prepare the salad jars to the end of step 4 the night before. Store peeled eggs in a separate container in the fridge.

PACK IT Pack egg separately to salad jar. Keep refrigerated until ready to eat.

1¼ cups (250g) farro
4 eggs
2 Lebanese cucumbers (260g), chopped coarsely
400g cherry tomatoes, halved
2 medium avocados (500g), chopped coarsely
½ cup (80g) smoked almonds
2 tbsps olive oil

PESTO DRESSING
⅓ cup store-bought basil pesto
2 tbsp lemon juice
⅓ cup extra virgin olive oil

1 Cook farro in a large saucepan of boiling water for 30 minutes or until tender; drain.

2 Make pesto dressing: Place pesto, lemon juice and extra virgin olive oil in a screw-top jar; season to taste. Shake well.

3 Meanwhile, place eggs in a small saucepan, cover with cold water; bring to the boil. Cook for 3 minutes or until soft-boiled; drain. Rinse under cold water; drain.

4 Spoon pesto evenly into four 1½ cup (375ml) glass jars; top with farro, cucumber, tomatoes, avocado, almonds.

5 Peel eggs, cut in half and place on top of each salad. Drizzle with oil. Season with cracked black pepper.

GREEK SALAD IN A JAR

PREP time 15 minutes

SERVES 2

PREP IT Make salad jars and dressing in the jar, the night before. Store all jars in the fridge.

PACK IT Pack salad jar and dressing jar separately to extra oregano. Keep refrigerated until ready to eat.

250g cherry tomatoes, halved
⅓ cup (80g) pitted kalamata olives
2 Lebanese cucumbers (260g), chopped coarsely
¼ medium red onion (45g), chopped coarsely
150g fetta, cut into 1cm cubes
¼ cup (60ml) extra virgin olive oil
2 tbsp red wine vinegar
2 tsp oregano leaves, chopped, plus extra leaves to serve (optional)

1 Divide tomatoes, olives, cucumber, onion and fetta between two 2½-cup (625ml) jars or airtight containers.

2 For the dressing, place oil, vinegar and chopped oregano in a screw-top jar; season to taste. Shake well.

3 Before serving, top with extra oregano leaves and drizzle with dressing.

STORE IT
Cookies will keep in an airtight container for up to 4 days.

OAT COOKIES

BASIC OAT COOKIES

PREP + COOK TIME 35 minutes (+ refrigeration)
MAKES 24

Preheat oven to 180°C/160°C fan-forced. Grease and line two oven trays with baking paper. Beat 250g softened butter and ¾ cup brown sugar in a bowl with an electric mixer until light and fluffy. Beat in 2 egg yolks and 1 tsp vanilla extract until combined. Stir in 1½ cups plain flour, 1 cup rolled oats, ¾ cup shredded coconut, ½ tsp bicarbonate of soda and ½ tsp salt; mix well. Roll 1½-tbsp portions of mixture into balls to make 24 in total. Place on trays 5cm apart; flatten into 6cm rounds. Refrigerate for 30 minutes. Bake for 20 minutes until golden. Cool on trays.

MUESLI COOKIES

PREP + COOK TIME 35 minutes (+ refrigeration)
MAKES 24

Make Basic Oat cookies (see recipe, above), omitting the oats and instead adding 1 cup nut-free fruit muesli and 1 tsp ground cinnamon with the dry ingredients. Roll 1½-tbsp portions of mixture into balls to make 24 in total. Place on trays 5cm apart; flatten into 6cm rounds. Refrigerate for 30 minutes. Bake for 20 minutes until golden. Cool on trays.

RASPBERRY OAT COOKIES

PREP + COOK TIME 35 minutes (+ refrigeration)
MAKES 24

Make Basic Oat cookies (see recipe, left), folding 125g frozen raspberries through the cookie mixture. Roll 1½-tbsp portions of mixture into balls to make 24 in total. Place on trays 5cm apart; flatten into 6cm rounds. Refrigerate for 30 minutes. Top cookie rounds with an extra 60g frozen raspberries, pressing in slightly. Bake for 20 minutes until golden. Cool on trays.

APRICOT OAT COOKIES

PREP + COOK TIME 35 minutes (+ refrigeration)
MAKES 24

Make Basic Oat cookies (see recipe, above left), adding ¾ cup chopped soft and juicy dried apricots with the dry ingredients. Roll 1½-tbsp portions of mixture into balls to make 24 in total. Place on trays 5cm apart; flatten into 6cm rounds. Refrigerate for 30 minutes. Bake for 20 minutes until golden. Top cookies with an extra ¼ cup thinly sliced soft and juicy dried apricots during the last 5 minutes of cooking, pressing in slightly. Cool on trays.

HOT STUFF

AIR FRYER ALL-DAY BURRITO BOWL

PREP + COOK TIME 40 minutes

SERVES 2

TIPS Use a heatproof dish such as a cake pan or ceramic dish. If you have a small air fryer, you may be able to create a bowl shape with the tortilla in the basket without using a dish.

1 small yellow capsicum (150g), sliced thinly
1 small green capsicum (150g), sliced thinly
2 tsp extra virgin olive oil
2 tsp mild taco seasoning
4 eggs
⅓ cup (35g) grated tasty cheese
50g ham, torn
⅓ cup (85g) mild taco sauce
2 large (22cm) tortilla wraps
guacamole, sour cream, coriander sprigs, sliced red chilli and lime wedges, to serve

1 Preheat a 7-litre air fryer to 180°C for 3 minutes.

2 Combine capsicums, oil and taco seasoning in a medium bowl. Taking care, place capsicum mixture in the air fryer basket; at 180°C, cook for 5 minutes or until softened. Transfer to a plate.

3 Meanwhile, in the same bowl, beat eggs using a fork, then add cheese, ham and taco sauce; season.

4 Press a tortilla wrap into an 18cm heatproof dish (see tips) to form a bowl shape; add half the egg mixture and half the capsicum mixture. Taking care, lower dish into the air fryer basket; at 180°C, cook for 12 minutes or until egg is just cooked through. Remove dish from the basket, then remove burrito bowl from the dish. Repeat with remaining tortilla wrap, egg mixture and capsicum mixture.

5 Top burrito bowls with guacamole, sour cream, coriander sprigs and sliced chilli; season with black pepper. Serve with lime wedges.

AIR
FRYER

AIR
FRYER

AIR FRYER SAUSAGE BUNS

PREP + COOK TIME 35 minutes

MAKES 6

PREP IT Sausage buns can be made the day before; store in an airtight container in the fridge. Reheat before serving.

2 x 250g fresh dough balls
6 pork sausages (500g)
olive oil cooking spray
1 egg, beaten
2 tsp poppy seeds
tomato or barbecue sauce, to serve

1 Bring dough balls to room temperature in their packet.

2 Preheat a 7-litre air fryer to 180°C for 3 minutes.

3 Pierce sausages using a fork. Spray the air fryer basket with cooking spray. Taking care, place sausages in the basket; at 180°C, cook for 10 minutes or until cooked through. Set aside to cool.

4 Meanwhile, combine dough balls, then on a lightly greased, clean work surface, roll dough into a 12cm x 24cm rectangle. Cut lengthways into six strips.

5 Wrap one strip of dough around each sausage to form a spiral; press dough together on each end to firmly seal. Brush dough all over with egg and sprinkle with poppy seeds.

6 Spray the air fryer basket with cooking spray. Taking care, place half the sausage buns in the basket; at 180°C, cook for 8 minutes or until golden and cooked through. Transfer to a plate. Repeat cooking remaining sausage buns.

7 Serve sausage buns warm with sauce.

AIR FRYER PORK & NOODLE BALLS

PREP + COOK TIME 35 minutes

MAKES 24

PREP IT Noodles balls can be made 3 days ahead; store in an airtight container in the fridge or the freezer for up to 2 months. Thaw in the fridge overnight, then reheat. Make dipping sauce a day ahead; refrigerate in its jar.

PACK IT Pack noodle balls in a lunch container with dipping sauce in a small separate airtight container. Keep chilled until ready to eat; reheat if desired.

225g hokkien noodles
400g fatty pork mince
4 green onions, chopped finely
1 tbsp finely grated ginger
2 cloves garlic, crushed
¼ cup finely chopped coriander roots and stems
1½ tbsp fish sauce
1 tsp Chinese five spice powder
olive oil cooking spray
chopped coriander leaves, to serve (optional)

DIPPING SAUCE
⅓ cup (110g) sweet chilli sauce
2 tbsp lime juice
2 tbsp finely chopped coriander leaves and stems

1 Place noodles in a large bowl and cover with boiling water; stand for 5 minutes to soften. Rinse under cold water; drain. Pat dry with paper towel: cut into 4cm lengths.

2 Preheat a 7-litre air fryer to 180°C for 5 minutes.

3 Combine noodles, pork, green onion, ginger, garlic, coriander roots and stems, fish sauce and five spice powder in a large bowl. Roll rounded tablespoons of noodle mixture into 24 balls using wet hands.

4 Spray noodle balls generously with cooking spray. Taking care, place noodle balls in the air fryer basket; at 180°C, cook for 20 minutes, turning halfway through cooking, until golden and crisp.

5 Make dipping sauce: Place ingredients in a screw-top jar; shake well.

6 Scatter noodle balls with chopped coriander. Serve with dipping sauce.

AIR FRYER

SANDWICH
PRESS

PROSCUITTO & PARMESAN SANDWICH PRESS PIZZA

PREP + COOK TIME 10 minutes

MAKES 2

TIP Ideal if your workplace has a sandwich press. If it doesn't, or for kids to take to school, simply follow step 2 the night before, cut into slices and pack in the morning as is.

PREP IT Pizzas can be prepared to the end of step 2 the night before; store in an airtight container in the fridge.

PACK IT Pack prepped pizza bases, prosciutto, rocket, parmesan and olive oil, separately in airtight containers. Just before eating, toast prepped bases in sandwich press, and top with the fresh ingredients.

2 x 24cm store-bought pizza bases
2 x 50g sachets pizza sauce
150g mozzarella, sliced thinly
100g prosciutto slices
30g baby rocket leaves
⅓ cup (25g) shaved parmesan
extra virgin olive oil, for drizzling (optional)

1 Preheat a sandwich press.

2 Spread pizza bases with pizza sauce; scatter with mozzarella.

3 Toast prepared pizza bases, one at a time, in hot sandwich press, between sheets of baking paper, for 2 minutes or until golden.

4 Top pizzas with prosciutto, rocket and parmesan; drizzle with olive oil, to serve. Season to taste.

EMPANADA TOASTIES

PREP + COOK TIME 1 hour

MAKES 6

PREP IT Toasties can be made the day before; store in an airtight container in the fridge before reheating.

FREEZE IT Toasties can be frozen, between sheets of baking paper, in an airtight container for up to 1 month; thaw in the fridge before reheating.

1 egg
⅓ cup (80ml) olive oil
1 small onion, chopped finely
2 cloves garlic, crushed
½ tsp sweet paprika
½ tsp ground coriander
½ tsp ground cumin
½ tsp dried oregano
225g lean minced beef
2 vine-ripened tomatoes, chopped finely
⅓ cup (50g) pimento-stuffed green olives, chopped finely
12 sheets fillo pastry
1 cup (120g) grated cheddar

CHIPOTLE MAYONNAISE
½ cup (150g) whole-egg mayonnaise
1 tbsp chipotle sauce

1 Cook egg in a saucepan of boiling water for 9 minutes. Cool. Peel and chop coarsely.

2 Heat 1 tbsp of the oil in a frying pan over high heat; cook onion, stirring, for 2 minutes. Add garlic, paprika, coriander, cumin and oregano; cook 1 minute. Add beef; cook, stirring to break up any lumps, for 3 minutes or until browned and cooked through. Add tomato; cook, stirring, for 2 minutes or until liquid is evaporated.

3 Remove pan from heat; stir in egg and olives. Season. Cool slightly.

4 Make chipotle mayonnaise: Combine ingredients in a small bowl, stir until smooth.

5 Layer 2 pastry sheets, brushing each sheet with a little of the oil. Place ¼ cup beef mixture and 2 tbsp of the cheese in a corner of the pastry stack; fold opposite corner across filling to form a triangle. Fold any excess pastry over and tuck under triangle to enclose filling. Repeat with remaining pastry, oil, beef mixture and cheese to make 6 toasties in total.

6 Preheat a sandwich press.

7 Brush each toastie with a little more oil. Toast, in batches, in hot sandwich press for 7 minutes or until golden and crisp.

8 Cut empanada toasties in half. Serve with chipotle mayo. Top with coriander leaves, if you like.

FREEZER FRIENDLY
SANDWICH PRESS

FREEZER
FRIENDLY

CHEAT'S CHILLI CON CARNE

PREP + COOK TIME
1 hour 5 minutes

SERVES 6

TIP For kids, leave out the Mexican chilli powder.

PREP IT Make chilli to the end of step 3 up to 2 days ahead; store in an airtight container in the fridge.

FREEZE IT Chilli can be frozen for up to 2 months; thaw in the fridge before reheating.

PACK IT In the morning, reheat chilli in the microwave; transfer to a Thermos food flask. Pack avocado, coriander and lime wedges in an airtight container and tortilla strips separately.

2 tbsp olive oil
1 medium red onion, chopped finely
2 cloves garlic, sliced thinly
1 medium red capsicum, chopped finely
500g lean beef mince
2 tbsp tomato paste
½ tsp dried oregano
½ tsp Mexican chilli powder (see tip)
2 x 400g cans diced tomatoes
400g can red kidney beans, drained, rinsed
1 large avocado, mashed
coriander leaves, tortilla strips and lime wedges, to serve

1 Heat oil in a frying pan over medium-high heat. Add onion, garlic and capsicum; cook, stirring, for 3 minutes or until the onion softens.

2 Increase heat to high; add beef and cook, stirring to break up any lumps, for 5 minutes or until browned and cooked through. Stir in tomato paste, oregano and chilli powder; cook for 1 minute.

3 Add tomatoes; bring to the boil. Reduce heat to low; cook, covered, for 30 minutes. Stir in beans; cook for 15 minutes or until thickened. Season to taste.

4 Serve chilli topped with avocado and coriander leaves, with tortilla strips and lime wedges to the side.

BEEF TACO PIES

PREP + COOK TIME 55 minutes (+ cooling)

MAKES 12

TIP Heating the tortillas before lining them in the pan holes, will make them more pliable and prevent them from tearing.

PREP IT Taco filling can be made up to 2 days ahead; store in an airtight container in the fridge. Prepare the recipe to the end of step 5 the day before; store filled tortilla shells and Mexican salad in separate airtight containers in the fridge.

FREEZE IT Taco filling can be frozen for up to 2 months; thaw in the fridge before reheating.

PACK IT In the morning, top filled tortilla shells with the sour cream, avocado, Mexican salad and coriander leaves; pack into a lunch container. Keep chilled until ready to eat.

12 x 15cm white corn tortillas
1 cup (120g) grated cheddar
1 large avocado, mashed
½ cup (120g) sour cream
lime wedges, to serve

TACO FILLING
1 tbsp olive oil
1 small onion, chopped finely
500g beef mince
30g packet taco seasoning mix
400g can diced tomatoes
2 tbsp tomato paste

MEXICAN SALAD
1 trimmed corn cob
1 cup (80g) shredded red cabbage
125g cherry tomatoes, halved or quartered
2 tbsp coriander leaves

1 Preheat oven to 180°C/160°C fan-forced. Grease a 12-hole (⅓-cup/80ml) muffin pan.

2 Make taco filling: Heat oil in a large frying pan over medium-high heat; cook onion, stirring, for 5 minutes or until onion softens. Add beef; cook, stirring to break up any lumps with a wooden spoon, for 5 minutes or until browned. Stir in seasoning mix, tomatoes, paste and ⅓ cup (80ml) water; bring to the boil. Reduce heat to low; cook for 15 minutes or until thickened. Season to taste. Cool.

3 Meanwhile, wrap tortillas in paper towel; heat in the microwave on HIGH (100%) for 40 seconds (see tip). Keep warm in a clean tea towel. Line pan holes with tortillas, pressing into bases and sides. Bake for 8 minutes or until golden and crisp.

4 Divide taco filling evenly between tortilla shells in muffin pan; sprinkle over cheddar. Bake for 10 minutes or until cheddar melts. Transfer to a wire rack.

5 Meanwhile, make Mexican salad: Boil, steam or microwave corn until just tender. When cool enough to handle, cut kernels from cob. Combine corn, cabbage, tomatoes and coriander in a bowl.

6 Top pies with avocado, sour cream and Mexican salad. Serve with lime wedges.

CHICKEN & CORN NOODLE SOUP

PREP + COOK TIME 40 minutes

SERVES 4

PREP IT Make soup up to 2 days ahead; store in an airtight container in the fridge.

PACK IT In the morning, reheat soup in the microwave; transfer to a Thermos food flask.

2 tbsp olive oil
4 green onions, sliced thinly
1 tbsp finely grated ginger
2 cloves garlic, crushed
1 litre (4 cups) chicken stock
300g chicken breast fillet
300g can corn kernels, drained
110g vermicelli egg noodles, crushed lightly
1 tbsp soy sauce
2 egg whites, beaten lightly (optional)

1 Heat oil in a large saucepan over medium heat. Cook half the green onion, the ginger and garlic, stirring, for 2 minutes or until fragrant. Increase heat to high. Add stock and 2 cups (500ml) water; bring to the boil. Add chicken. Reduce heat to low. Cook, covered, for 15 minutes or until chicken is cooked through; remove chicken from pan with a slotted spoon. When cool enough to handle, shred chicken.

2 Return broth to the boil. Add shredded chicken, corn, noodles and soy sauce to pan; cook for 7 minutes or until the noodles are tender and chicken is heated through. Reduce heat to low. Gradually stir in egg white; cook for 1 minute or until egg white is set. Season to taste.

3 Serve soup topped with remaining green onion.

BUTTER CHICKEN

PREP + COOK TIME 40 minutes

SERVES 4

TIPS If you prefer your butter chicken a little spicy, use a spicy butter chicken simmer sauce. Make this recipe for dinner and use the leftovers for your lunch the following day.

PREP IT Make butter chicken to the end of step 3 up to 2 days ahead; store in an airtight container in the fridge or freeze for up to 1 month. Thaw in the fridge before reheating.

PACK IT In the morning, reheat butter chicken and rice, separately, in the microwave. Assemble rice and butter chicken in a Thermos food flask.

600g chicken thigh fillets
2 tbsp vegetable oil
1 medium onion, sliced thinly
450g jar butter chicken simmer sauce (see tips)
1 cup (120g) frozen peas
2 large tomatoes, diced
450g microwave basmati rice
¼ cup coriander leaves

1 Trim fat from chicken; cut into 2.5cm pieces.

2 Heat half the oil in a large heavy-based frying pan over high heat. Cook chicken, in batches, for 3 minutes or until browned all over; remove from pan.

3 Heat remaining oil in same pan; add onion and cook for 4 minutes or until onion softens. Return chicken to pan with simmer sauce and ½ cup (125ml) water. Bring to the boil, then reduce heat to low; cook for 20 minutes or until sauce thickens and is reduced by half. Stir through peas and tomato; cook for 5 minutes or until tomato softens slightly. Season to taste.

4 Reheat rice following packet instructions.

5 Top butter chicken with coriander. Serve with rice.

FREEZER
FRIENDLY

FREEZER
FRIENDLY

CURRIED BEEF TRIANGLES

PREP + COOK TIME 1 hour

MAKES 8

TIP We used frozen vegetable mix of peas, corn and carrot. If using a vegetable mix with chunkier vegetables, you will need to finely chop them.

PREP IT Make triangles up to 2 days ahead; store in an airtight container in the fridge. Or freeze for up to 2 months; thaw in the fridge, before reheating in the oven.

PACK IT Pack triangles, raita and salad leaves in separate airtight containers.

1 tbsp vegetable oil
1 small onion, chopped finely
2 tsp finely grated ginger
1 clove garlic, crushed
1 tbsp curry powder
250g beef mince
⅓ cup (80ml) coconut cream
1 cup mixed frozen vegetables (see tip), chopped finely
¼ cup finely chopped coriander
2 sheets frozen puff pastry, thawed
1 egg, beaten lightly
1 tbsp poppy seeds
cucumber raita and green salad leaves, to serve (optional)

1 Heat oil in large frying pan over medium-high heat. Add onion, ginger and garlic; cook, stirring, for 5 minutes or until onion softens. Add curry powder; cook, stirring, for 1 minute or until fragrant. Add beef; cook, breaking up any lumps with a wooden spoon, for 5 minutes or until browned. Add coconut cream and ¼ cup (60ml) water; bring to the boil. Reduce heat to low; cook for 15 minutes or until most of the liquid evaporates. Stir in vegetables; cook for 2 minutes or until heated through. Remove from heat; stir in coriander. Season to taste. Cool.

2 Preheat oven to 200°C/180°C fan-forced. Line two oven trays with baking paper.

3 Cut each pastry sheet into quarters. Spoon ¼ cup beef mixture in the centre of each square. Brush pastry edges with a little egg; fold pastry in half diagonally to enclose filling, pressing edges together with a fork to seal.

4 Place triangles on trays. Brush tops with remaining egg; sprinkle with poppy seeds. Bake for 15 minutes or until browned.

5 Serve triangles with raita and salad leaves, if you like.

SCROLL SENSATIONS

PREP + COOK TIME 40 minutes **MAKES** 9 per variation

BASIC DOUGH Preheat oven to 200°C/180°C fan-forced. Grease and line a 20cm square cake pan with baking paper. Sift 2 cups self-raising flour, ½ tsp bicarbonate of soda and 1 tsp salt into a bowl; rub in 50g chopped chilled butter with your fingertips. Add approximately 1 cup buttermilk and mix to a soft, sticky dough. Turn dough onto a floured surface; knead lightly until smooth. Roll into a 30cm x 40cm rectangle.

CHEESYMITE SCROLLS

Make basic dough above. Warm 1½ tbsp Vegemite in a microwave to soften; spread over dough. Scatter with ½ cup grated tasty cheese. Roll dough tightly from long side. Using a serrated knife, trim the ends; cut roll into nine slices. Place scrolls, cut-side up, in pan; scatter scrolls with another ½ cup cheese. Bake scrolls for 25 minutes or until cooked through. Cool in pan.

SPICED APPLE SCROLLS

Make basic dough above. Combine 2 coarsely grated apples, 2 tbsp brown sugar and ½ tsp ground cinnamon in a bowl. Scatter apple mixture over dough. Roll dough tightly from long side. Using a serrated knife, trim ends; cut roll into nine slices. Place scrolls, cut-side up, in pan; brush with 1 tsp milk. Bake scrolls for 25 minutes or until cooked through. Cool in pan.

HAWAIIAN PIZZA SCROLLS

Make basic dough above. Spread dough with ⅓ cup pizza sauce. Scatter with 150g coarsely chopped ham, ½ cup well-drained, dried and coarsely chopped canned pineapple and ½ cup grated pizza cheese. Roll dough tightly from long side. Using a serrated knife, trim the ends; cut roll into nine slices. Place scrolls, cut-side up, in pan; scatter scrolls with another ½ cup cheese. Bake scrolls for 25 minutes or until cooked through. Cool in pan.

BLUEBERRY & CHIA SEED SCROLLS

Make basic dough above. Combine 125g fresh blueberries, 1 tbsp caster sugar, 1 tbsp chia seeds and 1 tsp finely grated orange rind in a bowl. Scatter berry mixture over dough. Roll dough tightly from long side. Using a serrated knife, trim the ends; cut roll into nine slices. Place scrolls, cut-side up, in pan; brush with 1 tsp milk and sprinkle with 1 tbsp demerara sugar. Bake scrolls for 25 minutes or until cooked through. Cool in pan.

STICKY BEEF FRIED RICE

PREP + COOK TIME 30 minutes (+ refrigeration)

SERVES 4

TIPS You will need 1 cup (200g) uncooked white rice to yield 3 cups cooked rice. Rice is best cooked the day before; store in an airtight container in the fridge. Alternatively, use 450g microwave long grain rice. Make this recipe for dinner and use the leftovers for your lunch the following day.

PREP IT Make fried rice the day before; store in an airtight container in the fridge.

PACK IT In the morning, reheat fried rice in the microwave. Assemble fried rice, egg ribbons, remaining green onion and sesame seeds in a Thermos food flask.

500g beef rump steak, sliced thinly
½ cup (125g) honey, garlic & soy marinade
2 eggs
3 tsp sesame oil
1 bunch broccolini, trimmed, cut into 5cm lengths
2 medium carrots, chopped
3 cups cold cooked long grain white rice (see tips)
4 green onions, sliced thinly
1 tbsp sesame seeds, toasted

1 Place beef and marinade in a medium bowl; mix well to coat. Cover; refrigerate for 1 hour, turning occasionally.

2 Meanwhile, whisk eggs in a small bowl; season. Heat 1 tsp of the oil in a large wok or frying pan over high heat; add egg, swirling in pan to form a 20cm round. Cook for 1 minute or until just set. Transfer to a plate; cool slightly. Roll omelette into a log; thinly slice into ribbons.

3 Heat another teaspoon of the oil in wok; add beef, in batches, and stir-fry for 2 minutes or until browned and cooked through. Transfer to a heatproof bowl with any pan juices.

4 Add remaining oil to wok; stir-fry broccolini and carrot for 2 minutes or until just tender. Return beef to wok with pan juices, rice and half the green onion; stir-fry for 1 minute or until heated through.

5 Serve fried rice topped with egg ribbons, remaining green onion and sesame seeds.

SAUSAGE PASTA BAKES

PREP + COOK TIME 45 minutes

SERVES 4

PREP IT Make pasta bakes the day before; store, covered, in the fridge.

PACK IT In the morning, reheat pasta bakes in the microwave; transfer to a Thermos food flask.

2 tbsp olive oil
500g penne pasta
500g good-quality pork sausages
1 medium onion, sliced thinly
500g jar tomato basil pasta sauce
250g cherry tomatoes, halved
1 cup basil leaves
200g fresh mozzarella, torn

1 Preheat oven to 180°C/160°C fan-forced. Brush four 2-cup (500ml) ovenproof dishes with 1 tbsp of the oil.

2 Cook pasta in a large saucepan of salted boiling water following packet instructions until just tender; drain. Return pasta to pan.

3 Meanwhile, squeeze sausage meat from casings into small chunks into a medium bowl.

4 Heat remaining oil in a large frying pan over medium-high heat; cook onion for 3 minutes or until soft. Add sausage meat; cook, stirring occasionally, for 6 minutes or until browned. Stir in pasta sauce; bring to the boil. Reduce heat to low-medium; cook for 5 minutes or until liquid reduces and thickens. Stir through tomatoes and half the basil.

5 Add sausage mixture to pasta in pan; stir to combine. Spoon pasta mixture evenly among ovenproof dishes; top with mozzarella.

6 Bake for 20 minutes or until cheese melts. Scatter with remaining basil leaves to serve.

MEATBALL & RISONI SOUP

PREP + COOK TIME 45 minutes

SERVES 4

PREP IT Soup can be made up to 3 days ahead; store in an airtight container in the fridge. Or freeze it for up to 1 month; thaw in the fridge, then reheat in a microwave. The pasta may absorb some of the stock on standing; add a little boiling water to thin, if you like.

PACK IT In the morning, reheat soup in the microwave; transfer to a Thermos food flask.

500g pork and fennel sausages
½ cup (50g) fresh breadcrumbs
2 cloves garlic, crushed
⅓ cup (25g) finely grated parmesan
¼ cup finely chopped flat-leaf parsley
2 tbsp extra virgin olive oil
1 small onion, chopped finely
1 bunch cavolo nero, leaves picked, torn coarsely
2 litres (8 cups) chicken stock
1 cup (220g) risoni
1 tbsp chopped dill (optional)

1 Preheat oven to 200°C/180°C fan-forced. Grease and line a large oven tray.

2 Remove sausage meat from casings; discard casings. Place sausage meat, breadcrumbs, garlic, parmesan and half the parsley in a large bowl; season. Using clean hands, mix until sausage meat is broken down and ingredients are well combined. Roll heaped tablespoons of mixture to make 16 balls in total; spread across prepared tray. Bake meatballs for 25 minutes or until cooked through and golden brown.

3 Meanwhile, heat oil in a large heavy-based saucepan over medium heat. Cook onion, stirring, for 3 minutes or until softened. Add cavolo nero; cook, stirring, for 1 minute. Add chicken stock; bring to the boil.

4 Add risoni to pan; cook for 5 minutes or until just tender. Add meatballs, remaining parsley and dill. Season to taste.

FREEZER
FRIENDLY

FREEZER
FRIENDLY

CHEAT'S PEA & HAM SOUP

PREP + COOK TIME 35 minutes

SERVES 4

PREP IT Soup can be made to the end of step 3 up to 3 days ahead; store in an airtight container in the fridge. Or freeze for up to 3 months; thaw in the fridge, then reheat in a microwave. Continue from step 4.

PACK IT In the morning, reheat soup in the microwave; transfer to a Thermos food flask and continue with step 4.

2 tbsp olive oil
1 leek, white part only, sliced thinly
1 clove garlic, chopped finely
1 large potato (200g), chopped
1.5 litres (6 cups) chicken stock
6 cups (720g) frozen peas
⅔ cup mint leaves
300g leg ham, sliced thinly
snow pea tendrils, to serve (optional)

1 Heat 1 tbsp of the oil in a large heavy-based saucepan over low-medium heat; cook leek and garlic, stirring, for 3 minutes or until softened.

2 Add potato, stock and 1 cup (250ml) water; bring to the boil. Reduce heat to low-medium; cook, covered, for 10 minutes or until potato is tender. Add 5 cups (600g) of the peas; cook for a further 2 minutes or until peas are just tender. Remove pan from heat.

3 Add mint to soup; blend with a stick blender until smooth. Add remaining peas; stir over low-medium heat until hot. Season to taste. Reduce heat to low; cover to keep warm.

4 Meanwhile, heat remaining oil in a frying pan over medium heat; cook ham, stirring, for 2 minutes or until golden brown and crisp.

5 Top soup with ham; season to taste. Serve soup topped with snow pea tendrils, if you like.

PIZZA SCROLLS

PREP + COOK TIME 40 minutes

MAKES 9

TIP The pineapple must be drained well, otherwise it will make the scrolls soggy. Once the pineapple pieces have been drained from the can, pat them dry with paper towel.

PREP IT Scrolls can be made a day ahead; store in an airtight container in the fridge.

2 cups (300g) self-raising flour
½ tsp bicarbonate of soda
1 tsp salt
50g cold butter, chopped coarsely
¾ cup (180ml) buttermilk, approximately
2 tbsp pizza sauce
2 tbsp barbecue sauce
½ small red onion (50g), sliced thinly
½ small green capsicum (75g), sliced thinly
100g sliced pepperoni, chopped coarsely
½ cup (100g) well-drained pineapple pieces, chopped coarsely (see tip)
⅓ cup (55g) drained sliced kalamata olives
1 cup (120g) pizza cheese

1 Preheat oven to 200°C/180°C fan-forced. Oil a 22cm square cake pan.

2 Sift flour, bicarb and salt into a medium bowl; rub in butter with your fingertips. Add enough buttermilk to mix to a soft, sticky dough. Turn dough onto a floured surface; knead lightly until smooth. Roll dough into a 30cm x 40cm rectangle.

3 Spread dough with combined sauces; sprinkle with onion, capsicum, pepperoni, pineapple, olives and half the cheese. Roll dough tightly from long side. Using a serrated knife, trim the ends. Cut roll into 9 slices; place scrolls, cut-side up, in pan. Sprinkle scrolls with remaining cheese.

4 Bake scrolls for 25 minutes or until cooked through.

MAKE
AHEAD

MAKE AHEAD
FREEZER FRIENDLY

PORK & APPLE SAUSAGE ROLLS

PREP + COOK TIME 1 hour (+ refrigeration)

MAKES 36

PREP IT Sausage rolls can be made up to 3 days ahead; store in an airtight container in the fridge before reheating.

FREEZE IT Sausage rolls can be frozen between sheets of baking paper in an airtight container for up to 3 months, thaw in the fridge before reheating.

2 eschalots, chopped coarsely
1 medium fennel bulb, chopped coarsely
2 medium green apples, cored, grated
2 tbsp olive oil
1 medium carrot, grated
4 cloves garlic, chopped finely
1kg pork mince
⅓ cup finely chopped flat-leaf parsley
6 sheets frozen puff pastry, thawed
2 eggs, beaten lightly
3 tsp white sesame seeds
tomato sauce, to serve

1 Preheat oven to 200°C/180°C fan-forced. Grease two large oven trays; line with baking paper.

2 Process eschalots and fennel in a food processor, using the pulse button, until chopped finely. Place apple in a colander and squeeze out excess liquid.

3 Heat oil in a large heavy-based frying pan over medium heat; cook eschalots and fennel for 4 minutes or until golden. Add apple, carrot and garlic; cook for 2 minutes. Transfer mixture to a sieve; press down to remove excess liquid. Cool.

4 Place pork, parsley and vegetable mixture in a large bowl; season. With clean hands, mix until well combined.

5 Cut pastry sheets in half lengthways. Spoon ⅓ cup of the mince mixture lengthways along the centre of each pastry piece. Fold one long side of pastry over filling. Brush pastry flap with a little egg, then fold over to enclose filling. Refrigerate for 30 minutes.

6 Using a sharp knife, cut each roll into thirds. Make two shallow cuts in the top of each sausage roll to allow steam to escape.

7 Place rolls, seam-side down, on trays. Brush with egg and sprinkle with sesame seeds. Bake for 30 minutes or until pastry is puffed and golden and filling is cooked through. If not serving straight away, transfer to wire racks to cool. Serve with tomato sauce.

REUBEN JAFFLES

PREP + COOK TIME 10 minutes

MAKES 2

PREP IT Sandwiches can be made to the end of step 2 the night before; store in an airtight container in the fridge. Continue with step 3 just before serving.

4 slices light rye bread
30g butter, softened
2 tsp pistachio dukkah (optional)
8 slices Swiss cheese
6 slices pastrami
⅓ cup (35g) store-bought sauerkraut
2 tbsp thousand island dressing

1 Preheat a jaffle maker.

2 Place bread on a sheet of baking paper on a chopping board. Spread each slice with butter, then sprinkle each evenly with ½ tsp dukkah. Turn two slices so the buttered-side faces down; top each with 2 slices Swiss cheese, 3 slices pastrami, 2 tbsp sauerkraut and 1 tbsp dressing, then season to taste. Top with remaining Swiss cheese, then sandwich together with remaining bread slices, buttered-side facing up.

3 Toast sandwiches in hot jaffle maker for 4 minutes or until cheese is melted and bread is crisp and golden.

FAST

FAST
SANDWICH PRESS

CHEAT'S SPINACH & CHEESE GÖZLEME

PREP + COOK TIME 20 minutes

MAKES 2

PREP IT Gözleme can be made to the end of step 3 the night before; store in an airtight container in the fridge.

PACK IT Pack tzatziki, lettuce wedges and dill sprigs in separate airtight containers to gözleme. Just before eating, continue from step 4.

2 tsp olive oil
1 small red onion, chopped finely
1 clove garlic, crushed
200g baby spinach leaves, chopped coarsely
1 egg, beaten lightly
200g fetta, crumbled
1½ tbsp finely grated parmesan
2 tsp finely grated lemon rind
2 tbsp chopped dill, plus extra sprigs to serve (optional)
4 wholegrain tortillas
tzatziki, baby cos wedges, to serve (optional)

1 Heat oil in a large heavy-based frying pan over medium heat; cook onion, garlic and spinach, stirring, for 2 minutes or until softened. Transfer to a large bowl. Cool slightly.

2 Add egg, fetta, parmesan, lemon rind and dill to spinach mixture, then season with pepper; mix well to combine.

3 Divide filling mixture between 2 tortillas, spreading to cover; sandwich together with remaining tortillas.

4 Preheat a sandwich press.

5 Toast gözleme, one at a time, in hot sandwich press for 3 minutes or until cooked through and golden.

6 Cut gözleme into wedges and serve with tzatziki, cos lettuce wedges and extra dill sprigs, if you like.

CHEESY CHORIZO QUESADITAS

PREP + COOK TIME 25 minutes

SERVES 2

PREP IT Quesaditas can be made to the end of step 2 the night before; store in an airtight container in the fridge. Just before eating, continue from step 3.

1 tbsp olive oil
1 small red onion, chopped finely
2 cured chorizos, chopped finely
1 tsp smoked paprika
⅓ cup (80g) drained chopped roasted red capsicum
2 wholemeal pitta pockets
1 cup (100g) grated four cheese mix
30g baby spinach leaves

1 Heat oil in a medium frying pan over medium-high heat; cook onion, stirring, for 3 minutes or until softened. Add chorizo; cook for 2 minutes or until golden. Add paprika; cook for 30 seconds. Stir in capsicum; season to taste.

2 Warm pitta pockets in the microwave to refresh, then halve and split open. Fill each pocket half with a quarter of the cheese mix, chorizo mixture and spinach then remaining cheese mix.

3 Preheat a sandwich press.

4 Toast quesaditas, two halves at a time, in hot sandwich press for 4 minutes or until golden and crisp.

FAST
SANDWICH PRESS

NUT-FREE TRAIL MIX

INDIAN

PREP TIME 5 minutes **MAKES** 3 cups

Combine 1½ cups crispy noodles, ½ cup lightly crushed plain ready-to-eat mini pappadums, ½ cup soy crisps, ¼ cup sultanas and ¼ cup crunchy seasoned peas in a medium bowl. Store in an airtight container for up to 1 week.

JAPANESE

PREP TIME 5 minutes **MAKES** 3¼ cups

Combine 1⅔ cups baked bbq rice crackers, 1 cup puffed rice cracker bites, ¼ cup wasabi peas, ¼ cup tamari pepitas and a 5g packet chopped roasted seaweed nori snack in a medium bowl. Store in an airtight container for up to 1 week.

RECESS

PREP TIME 5 minutes **MAKES** 4 cups

Combine 1½ cups salted natural popcorn, 2 x 25g packets mini pretzels, ⅓ cup banana chips, ½ cup dried sweetened cranberries and ¼ cup pepitas in a medium bowl. Store in an airtight container for up to 1 week.

TREAT

PREP TIME 5 minutes **MAKES** 2½ cups

Combine 1 cup crispix honey pillows, ½ cup yoghurt-coated berry frugo's, ¼ cup dark choc chips, ¼ cup toasted coconut flakes and ¼ cup mini pink marshmallows in a medium bowl. Store in an airtight container for up to 1 week.

MAKE
AHEAD

TREATS

MAKE AHEAD
AIR FRYER

AIR FRYER BANANA CHOC CHIP MUFFINS

PREP + COOK TIME 50 minutes

MAKES 12

TIP You will need about 4 ripe bananas for this recipe.

PREP IT Muffins can be made up to 3 days ahead; store in an airtight container. Or freeze for up to 2 months; thaw in the fridge overnight.

1½ cups (225g) plain flour
1 tsp baking powder
1 tsp bicarbonate of soda
1½ tsp ground cinnamon
¾ cup (165g) firmly packed brown sugar
½ cup (125ml) vegetable oil
1 egg, beaten lightly
2 tbsp milk
1 tsp vanilla extract
350g mashed ripe banana (see tip)
⅓ cup (65g) dark, milk or white chocolate chips
12 slices banana

1 Preheat a 7-litre air fryer to 160°C for 5 minutes. Line a 6-hole (⅓-cup/80ml) silicone muffin pan by stacking 2 paper cases in each hole. Double stack 12 more paper cases and set aside.

2 Place flour, baking powder, bicarb, cinnamon and sugar in a medium bowl; stir to combine well using a whisk. Place oil, egg, milk and vanilla in a jug; lightly whisk until combined. Pour the wet ingredients over dry ingredients; add mashed banana and ¼ cup (45g) of the chocolate chips, then stir until just combined. Divide half the mixture evenly among paper cases in muffin pan. Top with half the remaining chocolate chips and a banana slice on each.

3 Taking care, place muffin pan in the air fryer basket; at 160°C, cook for 17 minutes or until a skewer inserted into the centre of a muffin comes out clean. Leave muffins in pan for 5 minutes before transferring to a wire rack to cool completely. Repeat with remaining double-stacked muffin cases, muffin mixture, chocolate chips and banana slices.

EASY GRANOLA BARS

PREP + COOK TIME 55 minutes

MAKES 20

PREP IT Granola bars can be made up to 1 week ahead; store in an airtight container.

125g unsalted butter, chopped coarsely
⅓ cup (75g) firmly packed brown sugar
2 tbsp honey
1½ cups (135g) rolled oats
½ cup (75g) self-raising flour
½ cup (75g) dried apricots, chopped finely
8 fresh medjool dates, pitted, chopped finely
¼ cup (50g) pepitas
¼ cup (35g) sunflower seeds
⅓ cup (25g) shredded coconut

1 Preheat oven to 160°C/140°C fan-forced. Grease an 18cm x 28cm slice pan; line base and sides with baking paper, extending paper 5cm over long sides.

2 Stir butter, sugar and honey in a medium saucepan over low heat until sugar dissolves; stir in remaining ingredients. Press mixture firmly into pan.

3 Bake for 40 minutes or until golden. Cool in pan before cutting into 20 bars.

MAKE
AHEAD

FREEZER
FRIENDLY

CHOC BEETROOT SLAB CAKE

PREP + COOK TIME 50 minutes

MAKES 18 pieces

PREP IT Slab cake can be made up to 5 days ahead; store in an airtight container. Or wrap individual pieces of cake in plastic wrap, freeze for up to 3 months.

2 large beetroot (400g), peeled
1 cup (250ml) buttermilk
¼ cup (60ml) vegetable oil
1½ tbsp apple cider vinegar
125g butter, softened
1½ cups (330g) caster sugar
2 eggs
2 tsp vanilla bean paste
2½ cups (375g) plain flour
¼ cup (30g) Dutch-processed cocoa powder
1½ tsp bicarbonate of soda
1 tsp fine sea salt

1 Preheat oven to 180°C/160°C fan-forced. Grease a 25cm x 37cm x 5cm deep baking tray; line base and sides with baking paper, extending paper 5cm over long sides.

2 Grate beetroot; you will need 2½ cups grated beetroot. Transfer to a food processor with buttermilk, oil and vinegar; process until as smooth as possible.

3 Beat butter and sugar in a medium bowl with an electric mixer until smooth and pale; add one egg at a time, beating well after each addition. With motor operating, beat in vanilla. Fold in beetroot mixture until combined.

4 Sift flour, cocoa powder, bicarb and salt over wet ingredients; stir until just incorporated. Do not over-mix. Spoon mixture into pan.

5 Bake cake for 30 minutes or until a skewer inserted into the centre comes out clean. Leave cake in pan for 5 minutes before transferring to a wire rack to cool completely. Cut into 18 pieces.

CHOCOLATE & COCONUT WEET-BIX SLICE

PREP + COOK TIME 35 minutes (+ cooling & refrigeration)

MAKES 24 squares

PREP IT Slice can be made up to 1 week ahead; store in an airtight container.

4 Weet-Bix, crushed
1¼ cups (185g) self-raising flour, sifted
½ cup (110g) brown sugar
½ cup (40g) desiccated coconut, plus 2 tbsp extra
¼ cup (25g) Dutch-processed cocoa powder
185g butter, melted

ICING
1 cup (160g) icing sugar mixture
2 tbsp Dutch-processed cocoa powder
20g softened butter
2 tbsp boiling water

1 Preheat oven to 180°C/160°C fan-forced. Grease a 20cm x 30cm slice pan; line base and sides with baking paper, extending paper 2cm over long sides.

2 Place Weet-Bix, flour, sugar, coconut, cocoa and butter in a large bowl; mix well to combine. Press Weet-Bix mixture into pan.

3 Bake slice for 25 minutes or until firm to touch. Cool in pan.

4 Meanwhile, make icing: Sift icing sugar and cocoa into a small bowl. Add butter and the boiling water; mix until smooth.

5 Spread icing over cooled slice; sprinkle with extra coconut. Refrigerate for 30 minutes or until icing sets.

6 Transfer slice to a chopping board; cut into 24 squares.

MAKE
AHEAD

MAKE
AHEAD

RASPBERRY-CHIA COCONUT SLICE

PREP + COOK TIME 50 minutes (+ standing)

MAKES 18 bars

PREP IT Slice can be made up to 5 days ahead; store in an airtight container.

90g butter, softened
½ cup (110g) caster sugar
1 egg
⅔ cup (100g) plain flour
⅓ cup (50g) self-raising flour

RASPBERRY-CHIA JAM
250g fresh or frozen raspberries
1 tbsp white chia seeds
2 tsp maple syrup

COCONUT TOPPING
2 eggs
2 cups (160g) desiccated coconut
⅓ cup (75g) caster sugar

1 Make raspberry-chia jam: Process raspberries to a smooth puree; transfer to a small bowl. Stir in chia seeds and maple syrup. Stand for 20 minutes or until thickened.

2 Preheat oven to 180°C/160°C fan-forced. Grease a 18cm x 28cm slice pan; line base and sides with baking paper, extending paper 5cm over long sides.

3 Meanwhile, beat butter, sugar and egg in a small bowl with an electric mixer until light and fluffy. Stir in sifted flours in two batches. Spread mixture over base of pan, then spread raspberry-chia jam evenly on top.

4 Make coconut topping: Lightly beat eggs with a fork; stir in coconut and sugar until well combined. Spread topping over jam layer.

5 Bake slice for 35 minutes or until base is cooked and top is golden. Cool in pan before cutting into 18 bars.

STORE IT
Place blissful logs in an airtight container; store in the fridge for up to 1 week. Or freeze for up to 1 month.

BLISSFUL LOGS

GAYTIME

PREP TIME 20 minutes (+ refrigeration)
MAKES 10

Process 380g pitted fresh medjool dates until a thick paste forms. Transfer to a medium bowl with 1½ cups toasted rolled oats, ½ cup shredded coconut and 1 tsp vanilla extract; mix well to combine. Using damp hands, roll 2 level tablespoon portions of mixture into logs. Roll logs in ⅔ cup toasted buckwheat groats (kernels). Place on a baking-paper-lined oven tray. Refrigerate for 1 hour or until firm.

LEMON DELIGHT

PREP TIME 20 minutes (+ refrigeration)
MAKES 14

Process 2 cups each toasted rolled oats and desiccated coconut, 2 tbsp grated lemon rind, ⅓ cup lemon juice, ⅔ cup maple syrup and 1 tsp vanilla extract until mixture just starts to clump together. Using damp hands, roll 2 level tablespoon tbsp portions of mixture into logs. Roll logs in extra ½ cup desiccated coconut. Place on a baking-paper-lined oven tray. Refrigerate for 1 hour or until firm.

CARROT CAKE

PREP TIME 20 minutes (+ refrigeration)
MAKES 10

Coarsely grate 2 large carrots; you need 2 cups. Place grated carrot in a clean tea towel or piece of muslin; squeeze out as much liquid as possible. Combine carrot, 100g coarsely chopped pitted fresh medjool dates, 2 tsp cinnamon, ½ tsp ground ginger, ⅔ cup coarsely chopped dried apple, ¼ cup toasted rolled oats and 2 tbsp melted coconut oil in the bowl of a food processor; pulse until mixture just starts to clump together. With damp hands, roll 2 level tablespoon portions of mixture into logs. Roll logs in combined extra ½ cup toasted rolled oats and extra ½ tsp cinnamon. Place on a baking-paper-lined oven tray. Refrigerate for 1 hour or until firm.

CHERRY RIPE

PREP TIME 25 minutes (+ refrigeration)
MAKES 18

Thaw 2 cups frozen cherries on paper towel; pat dry. Place cherries, 3 cups toasted rolled oats, ⅓ cup maple syrup, 2 tbsp melted coconut oil, 2 tbsp white chia seeds, 1 cup moist coconut flakes and ⅓ cup finely chopped cranberries in the bowl of a food processor; pulse until mixture just starts to clump together. Using damp hands, roll 2 level tablespoon portions of mixture into logs. Place on a baking-paper-lined oven tray. Refrigerate for 1 hour or until firm. Meanwhile, place 150g dark chocolate in a microwave-safe bowl. Microwave on HIGH (100%) in 30-second bursts, stirring, until melted and smooth. Cool slightly. Dip log ends, one at a time, in chocolate, then sprinkle with extra moist coconut flakes. Return to baking-paper-lined oven tray. Stand at room temperature until chocolate sets.

APRICOT ORANGE BLOSSOM SQUARES

PREP TIME 15 minutes (+ refrigeration)

MAKES 20 squares

PREP IT Squares can be made up to 1 week ahead; store in an airtight container.

400g dried apricots
2 cups (160g) desiccated coconut
2 cups (320g) unsalted roasted cashews
1 cup (120g) almond meal
½ cup (40g) quinoa flakes or oat flakes
2 tbsp white chia seeds
¼ cup (70g) coconut yoghurt
2 tbsp orange blossom water
2 tbsp lemon juice
2 tbsp honey
½ cup (35g) shaved coconut, toasted (optional)

1 Line a 20cm square cake pan with baking paper, extending paper 5cm over long sides.

2 Process ingredients, except shaved coconut, until finely chopped and combined; mixture should clump together and start to come away from the side of the bowl.

3 Press apricot mixture into pan, using the back of a large spoon to spread out evenly to the edges; scatter with shaved coconut. Cover with plastic wrap and refrigerate for 1 hour to firm.

4 Transfer slice to a chopping board; cut into 20 squares.

MAKE
AHEAD

MAKE
AHEAD

SALTED CARAMEL THUMB PRINT COOKIES

PREP + COOK TIME 30 minutes

MAKES 22

PREP IT Cookies can be made up to 3 days ahead; store in an airtight container.

125g butter, softened
1 cup (120g) almond meal
½ cup (110g) caster sugar
½ teaspoon vanilla extract
1 egg
1 cup (150g) plain flour
¼ cup (70g) caramel top 'n' fill
1 teaspoon sea salt flakes

1 Preheat oven to 180°C/160°C fan-forced. Line two large oven trays with baking paper.

2 Place butter, almond meal, sugar and vanilla in the bowl of an electric mixer; beat on medium speed until light and fluffy. Add egg; beat until just combined. Sift over flour; fold in until well combined.

3 Using hands, roll 1-tbsp portions of mixture into balls to make 22 in total; place on trays 5cm apart. Press your thumb gently into the middle of each ball to make an indent.

4 Place caramel top 'n' fill and salt in a small bowl; mix well until smooth and combined. Fill each indent with ¼ tsp of the salted caramel.

5 Bake cookies for 12 minutes or until lightly golden. Leave on trays for 5 minutes before transferring to a wire rack to cool completely.

ANZAC BISCUITS

PREP + COOK TIME 45 minutes

MAKES 32

TIPS Spray your measuring spoon with a little cooking oil spray before scooping up the golden syrup; this will help prevent the syrup from sticking to the spoon. Make sure you use rolled oats rather than quick-cooking oats as they will produce a different result.

PREP IT Biscuits can be made up to 1 week ahead; store in an airtight container.

125g butter, chopped
2 tbsp golden syrup or treacle (see tips)
½ tsp bicarbonate of soda
2 tbsp boiling water
1 cup (90g) rolled oats (see tips)
1 cup (150g) plain flour
1 cup (220g) firmly packed brown sugar
¾ cup (60g) desiccated coconut

1 Preheat oven to 180°C/160°C fan-forced. Grease large oven trays; line with baking paper.

2 Stir butter and golden syrup in a medium saucepan over low heat until smooth. Stir in combined bicarb and the water, then remaining ingredients.

3 Roll level tablespoons of mixture into balls; place 5cm apart on lined trays, then flatten slightly.

4 Bake biscuits for 15 minutes or until golden. Cool biscuits on trays.

MAKE
AHEAD

MAKE
AHEAD

VANILLA CUPCAKES

PREP + COOK TIME 40 minutes

MAKES 24

PREP IT Cupcakes can be made up to 3 days ahead; store (without the icing sugar) in an airtight container.

125g butter, softened
1 tsp vanilla extract
¾ cup (150g) caster sugar
3 eggs
2 cups (300g) self-raising flour
¼ cup (60ml) milk
icing sugar, to dust (optional)

1 Preheat oven to 180°C. Line a 12-hole (⅓ cup/80ml) muffin pan with paper cases.

2 Beat ingredients, except icing sugar, in a medium bowl with electric mixer on low speed until ingredients are combined. Increase speed to medium; beat until mixture has changed to a paler colour. Spoon mixture into cases.

3 Bake cupcakes for 30 minutes or until a skewer inserted into the centre comes out clean. Leave in pan for 5 minutes before transferring to a wire rack to cool.

4 Serve cupcakes dusted with icing sugar.

BERRY JAM & ALMOND PALMIERS

PREP + COOK TIME 30 minutes (+ freezing & cooling)

MAKES 46

TIP Omit the almonds to make it nut-free and school friendly.

STORE IT Palmiers will keep in an airtight container for up to 3 days

½ cup (60g) flaked almonds, chopped very finely (see tip)
1 tsp vanilla bean paste
1 tsp finely grated orange rind
⅔ cup (215g) berry jam
2 sheets puff pastry
2 tbsp caster sugar

1 Combine almonds, vanilla, rind and jam in a small bowl.

2 Spread jam mixture evenly over pastry sheets. Fold two opposite sides of pastry inwards to meet in the middle; flatten slightly. Repeat fold again and flatten slightly. Fold again so the outside edges of pastry meet. Roll pastry in sugar, then wrap each roll, separately, in plastic wrap; freeze 30 minutes or until slightly firm.

3 Preheat oven to 180°C. Line oven trays with baking paper.

4 Remove then discard plastic wrap from pastry rolls; cut pastry into 1cm slices. Place slices, cut-side up, 5cm apart on trays.

5 Bake palmiers for 20 minutes or until puffed and golden. Cool on trays.

MAKE AHEAD
GLUTEN FREE

LAMINGTON CHIA PUDDING JARS

PREP TIME 25 minutes (+ overnight refrigeration)

SERVES 4

PREP IT Make the recipe up to the end of step 1 the day before. Spoon pudding mixture into the jars; cover with lids or plastic wrap. Place in an airtight container in the fridge overnight.

PACK IT In the morning, continue from step 2.

1 cup (250ml) coconut milk
½ cup (40g) shredded coconut, plus extra to serve
¼ cup (40g) white chia seeds
⅓ cup (80ml) maple syrup
2 tbsp cocoa powder
250g fresh raspberries
1 cup (180g) coconut yoghurt
½ cup gluten-free cocoa bombs

1 Whisk coconut milk, shredded coconut, chia seeds, maple syrup and 1 tbsp of the cocoa powder in a large bowl until well combined. Cover; refrigerate overnight or until thickened.

2 Reserve 12 of the raspberries; mash remaining raspberries in a small bowl.

3 Spoon chia mixture evenly among four 1-cup (250ml) jars; dust with a little of the remaining cocoa powder. Divide yoghurt among jars; top with the crushed raspberries and cocoa bombs. Scatter with extra shredded coconut and reserved raspberries.

BLUEBERRY GRANOLA PIE IN A JAR

PREP TIME 25 minutes (+ standing)

SERVES 4

TIP Use your favourite nut-free granola to make it nut free and school friendly.

250g fresh blueberries
2 medium yellow peaches (300g), cut into 2cm pieces
1 medium apple (150g), cut into 2cm pieces
1 tsp ground cinnamon
1 tsp vanilla bean paste
1 tsp finely grated lemon rind
⅓ cup (80ml) pure maple syrup
3 cups (360g) almond hazelnut granola (see tip)
2 cups (560g) Greek yoghurt

1 Place blueberries, peaches, apple, cinnamon, vanilla, lemon rind and 2 tbsps maple syrup in a medium bowl; stir to combine. Cover; stand for 30 minutes.

2 Meanwhile, process granola until coarsely chopped. Add remaining maple syrup; pulse until just combined.

3 Divide fruit mixture among four 1½-cup (375ml) jars; top with granola mixture. Serve with yoghurt.

SLICE & BAKE BISCUITS

PREP + COOK TIME 1 hour 30 minutes (+ refrigeration) **MAKES** 48

Beat 250g softened butter, 1¼ cups (200g) icing sugar and 2 tsp vanilla extract in a large bowl with an electric mixer until pale and fluffy. Stir in combined sifted 2 cups (300g) plain flour, ½ cup (75g) rice flour and ⅓ cup (50g) cornflour, in two batches, then 2 tbsp milk until mixed well. Divide mixture in half. Knead each half on a floured surface until smooth; roll halves into 25cm logs. Wrap each log in baking paper; refrigerate for 1 hour until firm or for up to 2 days. Preheat oven to 160°C. Grease oven trays. Cut logs into 1cm slices; place rounds 3cm apart on oven trays. Bake biscuits for 20 minutes or until pale golden, turning trays halfway through baking. Stand biscuits on trays for 20 minutes, before transferring to wire racks to cool. Dust biscuits with a little extra icing sugar before serving, if you like.

M&M'S

Make Slice-&-Bake Biscuits above, adding in 230g M&M's mini baking bits with the combined sifted flours, in batches. Continue as directed in the recipe.

TIP Colour from the M&M's may bleed a little into the dough.

ORANGE & POPPY SEED

Make Slice-&-Bake Biscuits above, omitting the vanilla extract and beating in 1 tbsp finely grated orange rind with the butter and icing sugar; add 1½ tbsp poppy seeds with combined sifted flours. Continue as directed in the recipe.

LEMON & PISTACHIO

Make Slice-&-Bake Biscuits above, omitting the vanilla extract and beating in 1 tbsp finely grated lemon rind with butter and icing sugar. Stir in ¾ cup (110g) roasted chopped pistachios with the combined sifted flours. Continue as directed in the recipe.

CINNAMON & PECAN

Make Slice-&-Bake Biscuits above, adding 1 tsp ground cinnamon to sifted flours and stirring in 1 cup (100g) roasted chopped pecans. Before baking, sprinkle sliced biscuits with 2 tbsp cinnamon sugar. Continue as directed in the recipe.

GLOSSARY

BREADCRUMBS
fresh bread processed into crumbs.
panko also known as Japanese breadcrumbs. Available in two types: larger pieces and fine crumbs. Both are lighter in texture than Western-style breadcrumbs. They are available from Asian grocery stores and most supermarkets.
stale crumbs made by grating, blending or processing 1- or 2-day-old bread.

BROCCOLINI a cross between broccoli and Chinese kale; it has long asparagus-like stems with a long loose floret, all are edible. Resembles broccoli but is milder and sweeter in taste.

BUTTERMILK originally the term given to the slightly sour liquid left after butter was churned from cream, today it is made from no-fat or low-fat milk to which specific bacterial cultures have been added. Despite its name, it is actually low in fat.

CHEESE
bocconcini from the diminutive of 'boccone', meaning 'mouthful' in Italian; walnut-sized, baby mozzarella, a delicate, semi-soft, white cheese traditionally made from buffalo milk. Sold fresh, it spoils rapidly so will only keep, refrigerated in brine, for 1 or 2 days at the most.
cheddar the most common cow's milk 'tasty' cheese; should be aged, hard and have a pronounced bite.
cream commonly called philadelphia or philly; a soft cow's milk cheese, its fat content ranges from 14% to 33%.
fetta Greek in origin; a crumbly textured goat's or sheep's milk cheese with a sharp, salty taste. Ripened and stored in salted whey; particularly good cubed and tossed into salads.
haloumi a firm, cream-coloured sheep's milk cheese matured in brine; it can be grilled or fried, briefly, without breaking down. Should be eaten warm as it becomes rubbery on cooling.
mozzarella soft, spun-curd cheese; originating in southern Italy where it was traditionally made from water-buffalo milk. Now generally made from cow's milk, it is the most popular pizza cheese because of its low melting point and elasticity when heated.
parmesan also called parmigiano; is a hard, grainy cow's milk cheese originating in the Parma region of Italy. The curd for this cheese is salted in brine for a month, then aged for up to 2 years.
pizza cheese a blend of grated mozzarella, cheddar and parmesan cheeses.
ricotta a soft, sweet, moist, white cow's milk cheese with a low fat content and a slightly grainy texture. The name roughly translates as 'cooked again' and refers to ricotta's manufacture from a whey that is itself a by-product of other cheese-making.

CHIA SEEDS contain protein and all the essential amino acids, as well as being fibre rich and a wealth of vitamins, minerals and antioxidants.

CHICKPEAS irregularly round, sandy-coloured legumes. Have a firm texture even after cooking, a floury mouth-feel and robust nutty flavour; available canned or dried (soak for several hours in cold water before use).

CHILLI generally, the smaller the chilli, the hotter it is. Use rubber gloves when seeding and chopping fresh chillies as they can burn your skin. Removing seeds and membranes lessens the heat level.
flakes also sold as crushed chilli; dehydrated deep-red extremely fine slices and whole seeds.

CINNAMON available in the piece (called sticks or quills) and ground into powder; one of the world's most common spices, used universally as a sweet, fragrant flavouring for both sweet and savoury foods.

COCOA POWDER also called unsweetened cocoa; cocoa beans (cacao seeds) that have been fermented, roasted, shelled, ground into powder then cleared of most of the fat content.
Dutch-processed is treated with an alkali to neutralise its acids. Reddish-brown in colour, it has a mild flavour and easily dissolves in liquids.

COCONUT
cream obtained commercially from the first pressing of the coconut flesh alone, without the addition of water; the second pressing (less rich) is sold as coconut milk.
desiccated concentrated, dried, unsweetened and finely shredded coconut flesh.
flaked dried flaked coconut flesh.
milk not the liquid inside the fruit (coconut water) but the diluted liquid from the second pressing of the white flesh of a mature coconut. Available in cans and cartons at supermarkets.
shredded unsweetened thin strips of dried coconut flesh.

CORIANDER a bright-green leafy herb with a pungent flavour. Both stems and roots of coriander are also used in cooking; wash well before using. Also available ground or as seeds; these should not be substituted for fresh as the tastes are completely different.

CORNFLOUR made from corn (maize) or wheat (wheaten cornflour gives a lighter texture in cakes); used as a thickening agent in cooking.

CRANBERRIES available dried and frozen; have a rich, astringent flavour and can be used in sweet and savoury dishes. The dried version can usually be substituted for or with other dried fruit.

CUMIN also known as zeera or comino; resembling caraway in size, cumin is the dried seed of a plant related to the parsley family.

CURRY POWDER a blend of ground spices used for making Indian and some South-East Asian dishes. It consists of dried chilli, cumin, cinnamon, coriander, fennel, mace, fenugreek, cardamom and turmeric. Available mild or hot.

EDAMAME are fresh soy beans in the pod; available frozen from Asian food stores and major supermarkets.

FLOUR
plain a general all-purpose wheat flour.
rice very fine, almost powdery, gluten-free flour; made from ground white rice. Used in baking, as a thickener, and in some Asian noodles and desserts.
self-raising plain flour sifted with baking powder in the proportion of 1 cup flour to 2 tsp baking powder.

GINGER
ground also called powdered ginger; used as a flavouring in baking but cannot be substituted for fresh ginger.
pickled pickled paper-thin shavings of ginger in a mixture of vinegar, sugar and natural colouring; can be pink or red coloured. Used in Japanese cooking. Available, packaged, from Asian food stores.

GOLDEN SYRUP a by-product of refined sugarcane; pure maple syrup or honey can be substituted. Treacle is a similar product, however, it is more viscous and has a stronger flavour and aroma; golden syrup has been refined further and contains fewer impurities.

HARISSA a Moroccan paste made from dried chillies, cumin, garlic, oil and caraway seeds. Available from Middle Eastern food shops and major supermarkets.

HUMMUS a Middle Eastern dip made from softened dried chickpeas, garlic, lemon juice and tahini; can be purchased ready-made from most delicatessens and supermarkets.

KIDNEY BEANS medium-sized red bean, slightly floury in texture yet sweet in flavour. Sold dried or canned; found in bean mixes and is used in chilli con carne.

MAPLE SYRUP distilled from the sap of sugar maple trees found only in Canada and the USA. Maple-flavoured syrup or pancake syrup are not adequate substitutes for the real thing.

MUSTARD
American bright yellow in colour, a sweet mustard containing mustard seeds, sugar, salt, spices and garlic. Commonly served with hot dogs and hamburgers.

Dijon pale brown, distinctively flavoured, fairly mild-tasting French mustard.
wholegrain also known as seeded mustard. A French-style coarse-grain mustard made from crushed mustard seeds and Dijon-style French mustard.

NORI a type of dried seaweed used in Japanese cooking as a flavouring, garnish or for sushi. Sold in thin sheets, plain or toasted (yaki-nori).

OIL
olive made from ripened olives. Extra virgin and virgin are the first and second press, respectively, of the olives; 'light' refers to taste not fat levels.
sesame made from toasted, crushed, white sesame seeds; used as a flavouring rather than a cooking oil.

ONION
eschalots also called shallots, French shallots or golden shallots; small and brown-skinned.
green also called, incorrectly, shallot; an immature onion picked before the bulb has formed. Has a long, bright-green edible stalk.
red also known as Spanish, red Spanish or Bermuda onion; a sweet-flavoured, large, purple-red onion.

PAPRIKA ground, dried, sweet red capsicum; there are many grades and types available, including sweet, hot, mild and smoked.

PASTRY SHEETS ready-rolled packaged sheets of frozen puff and shortcrust pastry, available from supermarkets.

PEPITAS are the pale green kernels of dried pumpkin seeds; available plain or salted.

POPPY SEEDS small, dried, bluish-grey seeds of the poppy plant with a crunchy texture and a nutty flavour. Available whole or ground from delicatessens and most supermarkets.

QUINOA (pronounced keen-wa) is cooked and eaten as a grain alternative but is in fact a seed. It has a delicate, nutty taste and chewy texture. It is gluten free.

ROASTING/TOASTING desiccated coconut, pine nuts and sesame seeds roast more evenly if stirred over low heat in a heavy-based frying pan; their natural oils will help turn them golden. Remove from pan immediately. Nuts and dried coconut can be roasted in the oven to release their aromatic essential oils. Spread evenly onto an oven tray, roast at 180°C for about 5 minutes

ROCKET also called arugula; a peppery green leaf mostly eaten raw in salads. Baby rocket leaves are smaller and less peppery.

SESAME SEEDS black and white are the most common of this small oval seed; also red and brown varieties. Used in cuisines around the world as an ingredient and as a condiment.

SPINACH also called english spinach and incorrectly, silver beet. Baby spinach leaves are eaten raw in salads or cooked until wilted.

SOY SAUCE made from fermented soy beans. Several variations are available.

SUGAR
brown very soft, finely granulated sugar retaining molasses for its colour and flavour.
caster finely granulated table sugar.
icing pulverised granulated sugar crushed together with a small amount of cornflour.
pure icing same as icing sugar but without the addition of cornflour; needs to be sifted.

SUMAC a purple-red, astringent spice, ground from berries growing on shrubs that flourish wild around the Mediterranean; adds a tart, lemony flavour. Available from most supermarkets.

TACO SEASONING MIX a packaged seasoning meant to duplicate the Mexican sauce made from oregano, cumin, chillies and other spices.

TAHINI a rich, sesame-seed paste.

TAMARI a thick, dark soy sauce made mainly from soy beans, but without the wheat used in most standard soy sauces.

VANILLA
extract obtained from vanilla beans infused in water; a non-alcoholic version of essence.
paste made from vanilla beans and contains real seeds. It is highly concentrated: 1 tsp replaces a whole vanilla bean.

ZUCCHINI also called courgette; small dark-green or yellow vegetable of the squash family.

CONVERSION CHART

MEASURES

One Australian metric measuring cup holds approximately 250ml; one Australian metric tablespoon holds 20ml; one Australian metric teaspoon holds 5ml. The difference between one country's measuring cups and another's is within a two- or three-teaspoon variance and will not affect your cooking results. North America, New Zealand and the United Kingdom use a 15ml tablespoon. All cup and spoon measurements are level.

The most accurate way of measuring dry ingredients is to weigh them.

When measuring liquids, use a clear glass or plastic jug with the metric markings.

We use extra-large eggs with an average weight of 60g.

DRY MEASURES

metric	imperial
15g	½oz
30g	1oz
60g	2oz
90g	3oz
125g	4oz (¼lb)
155g	5oz
185g	6oz
220g	7oz
250g	8oz (½lb)
280g	9oz
315g	10oz
345g	11oz
375g	12oz (¾lb)
410g	13oz
440g	14oz
470g	15oz
500g	16oz (1lb)
750g	24oz (1½lb)
1kg	32oz (2lb)

LIQUID MEASURES

metric	imperial
30ml	1 fluid oz
60ml	2 fluid oz
100ml	3 fluid oz
125ml	4 fluid oz
150ml	5 fluid oz
190ml	6 fluid oz
250ml	8 fluid oz
300ml	10 fluid oz
500ml	16 fluid oz
600ml	20 fluid oz
1000ml (1 litre)	1¾ pints

LENGTH MEASURES

metric	imperial
3mm	⅛in
6mm	¼in
1cm	½in
2cm	¾in
2.5cm	1in
5cm	2in
6cm	2½in
8cm	3in
10cm	4in
13cm	5in
15cm	6in
18cm	7in
20cm	8in
22cm	9in
25cm	10in
28cm	11in
30cm	12in (1ft)

OVEN TEMPERATURES

The oven temperatures in this book are for conventional and fan-forced ovens.

	°C (Celsius)	°F (Fahrenheit)
Very slow	120	250
Slow	150	300
Moderately slow	160	325
Moderate	180	350
Moderately hot	200	400
Hot	220	425
Very hot	240	475

Measurements for cake pans are approximate only. Using same-shaped cake pans of a similar size should not affect the outcome of your baking. We measure the inside top of the cake pan to determine size.

INDEX

Published in 2026 by Are Media Books, Australia.
Are Media Books is a division of Are Media Pty Ltd.

ARE MEDIA BOOKS

Chief Executive Officer Jane Huxley

Books Director David Scotto

Project Editor Stephanie Kistner

Senior Designer Kelsie Walker

Food Editor Bronwen Clark

Production Controller Kara Stead

The recipes in this book have previously appeared in other publications by Are Media.

Printed in China by
C&C Offset Printing Co. Ltd. China

A catalogue record for this book is available from the National Library of Australia.
ISBN 978-1-76122-214-6

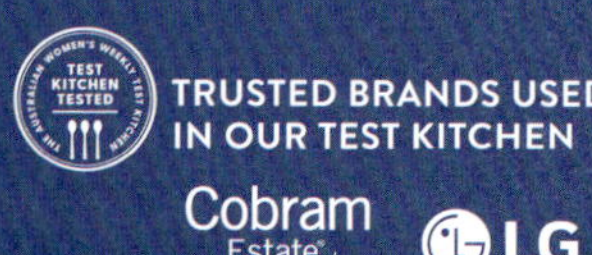

Published by Are Media Books, a division of Are Media Pty Limited, 54 Park St, Sydney; GPO Box 4088, Sydney, NSW 2001, Australia
Ph +61 2 9282 8000;
www.awwcookbooks.com.au

International rights enquiries
internationalrights@aremedia.com.au

Order books
phone 1300 322 007
(within Australia)

or order online at
www.awwcookbooks.com.au

Send recipe enquiries to
recipeenquiries@aremedia.com.au

 womensweeklyfood

 @womensweeklyfood